Mass Transit
Policy
Planning

Mass Transit Policy Planning

An Incremental Approach

William J. Murin
University of Wisconsin–Parkside

Heath Lexington Books
D.C. Heath and Company
Lexington, Massachusetts
Toronto   London

Table of Contents

List of Figures

List of Tables

Preface

Mass transit systems as typically designed have tended to serve only a minority of all urban travelers, the suburb to downtown commuter, and have almost entirely ignored the travel needs of other urban workers. Beginning with the 1965 McCone Commission Report on the Watts riots through the Report of the National Advisory Commission on Civil Disorders in 1968, it has become apparent that governmental transportation policy has left unserved a large group in the population who have a need for mass transit, the low income, inner city resident who works or could find a job in the suburbs—the reverse commuter. The decentralization of employment and the segregation of minority groups in the inner city has created a "mobility gap" in terms of access to employment and other urban services that is just now being fully realized. By assuming a homogeneous transportation public and almost universal ownership of an automobile, governmental transportation policy has ignored the consequences of such a policy on those who lack access to a car.

This research investigates some of the values and consequences of the transportation planning process operative in planning the rail rapid transit system (METRO) currently being constructed in the Washington, D.C. metropolitan area. Using the METRO system as a case study, this research combines empirical investigation and value consequences in an attempt to determine the impact of the transportation policy making process on the distribution of transit benefits.

From the transportation perspective, the major finding of this research is that Washington, D.C.'s inner city residents will not receive the same qualitative service from METRO as will other groups and interests, most notably the downtown business interests and the suburb to city commuters. From this perspective then, the McCone, Kerner, and other governmental sponsored studies relative to the transportation deprivation of the low income, have had little visible impact on the distribution of transit benefits to be realized from the National Capital area's METRO system.

From the policy making standpoint, a specific attempt was made to separate the process from the consequences with the result that incremental policy making in the METRO project did not allow for a comprehensive review of the service to be provided to low income, inner city residents.

Marginal (incremental) changes in the overall route structure of the system (the realignment of a part of the system or the elimination of a section of the system) resulted in large negative consequences to the low income residents of inner city Washington, D.C. Because the goals of the low income were not compatible with other expressed values and externally imposed constraints on the kind of transit service to be provided, inner city residents were not benefited by incremental policy making in transit policy.

From a broader viewpoint, the METRO experience demonstrates that change oriented values lost out to status quo oriented values in determining the nature and scope of the system. Even though the accommodation of the change oriented values would have permitted a wider distribution of the benefits to be realized from METRO, status quo values were able to predominate in determining who should and who would be served by METRO.

Acknowledgments

This research has been made possible by the efforts of several individuals. Professor Clarence N. Stone of the Department of Government and Politics, University of Maryland, directed the project and spent many hours reading the manuscript and offering helpful suggestions. Professor H. David Jenkins of Norfolk State College provided valuable technical assistance and made the statistical efforts manageable.

This writer must also thank the Urban Transportation Center of the Washington, D.C. Consortium of Universities and the Woodrow Wilson Dissertation Fellowship Program for the funds to enable him to complete this research.

Finally, my gratitude goes to my wife Judy whose spirit made bearable the times when progress was negligible, and for her proofreading and artistic efforts.

Obviously, any errors of fact or judgment are solely the responsibility of the author.

Mass Transit
Policy
Planning

1

Transportation and Job Decentralization: Implications for the Urban Disadvantaged

Wilfred Owen, in his work, *The Metropolitan Transportation Problem*,[1] notes that cities in all parts of the world are struggling to achieve some acceptable standard of mobility. Even where the automobile is scarce, modern and traditional means of transportation combine to create chaos and congestion not unlike that familiar to the American commuter.[2] Yet, while the commuter crisis may not be uniquely American, there are transportation problems that occur in a specifically American form, reflecting in particular our experience with race and poverty.

Growing affluence and residential dispersion have led many policy analysts to assume that we have a homogeneous transportation public.

Thus, since the end of World War II, the predominance of the private automobile as the preferred means of travel, and the rise of suburbia as the preferred dwelling pattern, have resulted in American transportation literature concentrating on the suburbanite's dependence on the automobile; analyzing his selection of the automobile as the preferred means of travel; lamenting the shortcomings of the public transportation system; editorializing that more freeways will not necessarily solve the problem; and finally presenting several recommendations for a balanced[a] transportation network, while calling for a closer working relationship between transportation and community planning.

With increased attention to the problems of poverty and race in our society, it has become apparent that services for an undifferentiated general public often have dire consequences for minorities. Effective transportation service requires adaptation to each clientele's social and economic conditions.

The research proposed here is, then, deliberately concerned with this new client-oriented perspective.[3] It focuses on service to groups with the most critical and often neglected needs—minority groups in the inner city. This research will not provide a comprehensive review of the METRO program from a regional development standpoint. It will examine the impact of METRO planning and policy making from the perspective of minority inner city residents.[4]

The McCone Commission Report on the 1965 Watts riots was the initial acknowledgment that governmental transportation policy had not served an important segment of the public. The Report emphatically stated that:

---

[a]The definition of "balanced" is usually modified to meet the needs of the user. For a highway planner, the concept has entirely different connotations than it does for advocates of rapid rail transit.

... inadequate and costly public transportation currently existing throughout the Los Angeles area seriously restricts the residents of the disadvantaged areas.... This lack of adequate transportation handicaps them in seeking and holding jobs, attending schools, shopping, and in fulfilling other needs. It has had a major influence in creating a sense of isolation, with its resultant frustrations, among the residents of south central Los Angeles, particularly of the Watts area.[5]

Isolation in an urban setting is much more than a psychological state affecting the sense of community. Transportation resources have a major impact on job opportunities and accessibility to those jobs; and it is employment that is recognized by the McCone Commission as "the most serious immediate problem that faces Negroes..." in the Los Angeles area.[6] Subsequent to the Watts findings, the relationship between inadequate transportation on one hand, and employment and isolation on the other, has become the subject of increasing concern in academic and governmental circles.

In most urban areas the mobility problem of the poor is not due to the absence of public transportation. Rather, research to date directs our attention to the changing nature of the urban area in which the minority poor live and work. For the most part, the poor continue to live in centrally located areas[b] that are reasonably well served by traditional public transportation to the central business district (CBD) where the highest density of jobs usually exists.

To the extent that the jobs of the minority poor are centrally located, the poor are mobile, and public transportation adequately serves their travel demands. The problem for the inner city resident arises when a centrally located firm decides to move its manufacturing, warehousing, or clerical activities from the central city to the suburbs. For the white worker, the change in job location usually presents no problem. If he lives in the city he can either move closer to his relocated job or use his automobile to commute to the new job site. If he already is a suburban resident, he may now be closer to his job and may no longer have to contend with morning and evening rush hours.

For the minority inner city resident however, all indications are that housing and transportation choices are more limited than they are for white workers. Housing market discrimination[c] in most suburban communities has prevented

---

[b]For both 1959 and 1964, the proportion of poor families was higher in central cities than in the suburbs. For 1964, the percentage of the population with an annual family income below $3000 was 15 percent in the city and 10 percent in the suburbs, as compared with 1959 figures of 18 percent in the city and 13 percent in the suburbs. U.S. Department of Commerce, Bureau of the Census, *Consumer Income*, Series P-60, Table 48 (April, 1966), p. 3.

[c]Even with the 1968 legislation barring racial discrimination in the sale or rental of housing, there does not seem to be much reason to expect that the housing patterns of minority group members will change greatly in the foreseeable future. Current research suggests that the decentralization of minority groups will occur only slowly, and probably only then by spreading out into older neighborhoods close to the center of the metropolitan area (Edgar M. Hoover and Raymond Vernon, *Anatomy of a Metropolis* (New York: Anchor Books, Doubleday and Company, 1962), pp. 215-229).

the minority group member from following his job to the suburbs;[7] and where adequate housing is available, it is usually priced above comparable housing for a white worker in the same income bracket.

The most complete study of the distribution and movement of jobs in metropolitan areas, based on data through 1958, found that most large cities are declining as employment centers.[8] An elaboration of this position using more recent data concluded that:

. . . most central parts of metropolitan areas are losing employment to outlying areas, and that this process is, if anything, increasing. Slow growth, and not infrequent declines of central cities, have accumulated to the point where absolute declines in central city employment are now commonplace.[9]

What we are essentially faced with is the realization that blue-collar and semiskilled jobs have decentralized far more rapidly than have housing opportunities for minority workers in those jobs.

Living in a central city neighborhood well serviced by public transportation to the central business district is less of an advantage for lower income groups than it once was. Little public transit exists to get the inner city resident to suburban jobs because traditional public transportation systems are not structured to provide adequate "reverse commuting" service.[d]

Our immediate concern here is the degree to which this pattern is true for the National Capital area. In terms of our major research question, if the kinds of jobs low income, semiskilled, inner city residents are likely to hold are leaving the city, then the transit link between home and job becomes extremely important.

The economy of the Washington, D.C. area is of considerable interest and some uniqueness because the National Capital area is one of the few metropolitan areas of its size (2.8 million in 1970) to have so large a proportion of its labor force in one industry. Just over one-third of all employment in the region is federal, with white collar and professional jobs making up much of the remainder.[e] For the nation as a whole, not quite 10 percent of the labor force is

[d]Sumner Myers, in "Personal Transportation for the Poor," *Interrelationships of Transportation and Poverty: Summary of Conference on Transportation and Poverty* (Brookline, Mass.: American Academy of Arts and Sciences, 1968), p. 9, argues that a "reverse" commuter relying on public transit can cover only one-third the distance he could cover by car in the same amount of time. This means that his potential labor market is one-ninth the size that it might otherwise be. Myers points out that a resident of southeast Washington, D.C. who can spend no more than one hour going to work by bus is limited to an area which provides 571,000 jobs. By car, he could reach any part of an area providing 865,000 jobs. Other things being equal, his job opportunities are half again as great by car as they are by bus. Other things are not equal however, as there are likely to be more of the inner city resident's kinds of jobs outside of the one hour by bus area—the outer suburbs.

[e]The Census Bureau defines the Washington, D.C.-Maryland-Virginia Standard Metropolitan Statistical Area (SMSA) as consisting of the District of Columbia, Montgomery and Prince Georges counties in Maryland, Alexandria, Fairfax, and Falls Church cities in Virginia, and Arlington, Fairfax, Loudoun, and Prince William counties in Virginia. The latter two Virginia counties were added to the SMSA in 1963 and are not included in any of the data in this research.

in the service category, while in Washington, D.C., it is 50 percent plus.[10] Heavy industry, trucking, and warehousing activities do not exist to any great extent in the region. The Washington, D.C. metropolitan area has been essentially a white collar and professional community.

The data presented in Table 1-1 show that the region's economy is based on government, retailing, and service categories. In 1954, these three sectors accounted for just over 70 percent of all regional employment while the 1967 figure was 71.6 percent.

In addition, several other items are noteworthy in the Table 1-1 data. Over the past decade and a half, federal government dominance of the region's economic base has declined in importance even though the government is still the largest single employer in the region. Service functions have had the greatest increase of any job category, public or private, while other non-governmental jobs have only marginally increased their share of regional jobs.

The decrease in the government's share of employment from 43.6 percent to 34.4 percent is not unexpected given the growth and diversification of the region over the past fifteen years. Population in the area in 1950 was 1.29 million, in 1960 it was 2.06 million, 2.83 million in 1970, and is projected to grow to 5.3 million by the year 2000.[11] With the population growth has come a broadening of the region's economic base so that the federal government now accounts for just over one-third of all employment.

The National Capital Planning Commission estimates that out of a labor force of 2.1 million in the year 2000, over 25 percent will be in the service industry. Although manufacturing cannot be expected to become a dominant force in the region, Table 1-2 shows that manufacturing jobs are expected to increase to 8.4 percent of all jobs by the end of the century, an increase of almost 130,000 jobs. All other categories are projected to decrease slightly in relative importance despite some rather respectable increases in absolute terms.

The employment base in the Washington, D.C. area provides three reasons why the national pattern of job decentralization may not be replicated (or may be copied to a lesser degree) here. First, the region has few manufacturing and wholesale types of jobs, the kinds of jobs that have led the movement from the city.[12] Thus the District of Columbia cannot lose a large part of its employment to the suburbs via these jobs. Second, the federal government as the largest single employer in the region affects the location of several hundreds of thousands of employees. The federal government, by keeping its labor force in the city, can do more to offset the decentralization of jobs than can any individual private sector employer, or perhaps any group of them.

Finally, the professional nature of much of the region's employment involves frequent face-to-face communications. Thus, consultants, trade organizations, research groups, public relations firms, and other companies who conduct much of their business with the government are constrained from either leaving the city or from moving too far out into the suburbs.[13] On the other hand, the

Table 1-1

**Employment in the Washington, D.C. Metropolitan Area
1954-1967 (In Thousands)**

Employment	1954	1958	1963	1967
Total	518	623	736	905
Federal	226	228	263	311
Private[a]	292	396	473	595
Manufacturing	30	35	50	49
Wholesale	20	23	30	36
Retail	80	93	124	145
Construction	35	46	48	62
Transportation/				
Utilities	31	39	37	50
F.I.R.E.[b]	34	39	43	61
Services	61	111	141	191

Percent of Total

Total	100.0	100.0	100.0	100.0
Federal	43.6	36.6	35.8	34.4
Private[a]	56.4	63.4	64.2	65.6
Manufacturing	5.8	5.6	6.8	5.4
Wholesale	3.8	3.7	4.0	3.9
Retail	15.5	14.9	16.8	16.0
Construction	6.8	7.4	6.5	6.9
Transportation/				
Utilities	6.0	6.3	5.0	5.6
F.I.R.E.[b]	6.5	6.3	5.9	6.8
Services	11.7	17.8	19.2	21.2

[a]Excluded are agriculture, mining, forestry, and fishing.

[b]Represents finance, insurance, and real estate.

Source: U.S. Department of Commerce, Bureau of the Census, *Census of Business: 1954, 1958, 1963,* Vol. 2, *Retail Trade,* area statistics, Parts 1 & 2, Vol. 4, *Wholesale Trade,* area statistics; *Census of Business: 1967, Retail Trade,* area statistics (preprint), *Wholesale Trade,* area statistics (preprint); *Census of Manufacturers: 1954, 1958, 1963,* Vol. 3, area statistics; *County Business Patterns: 1953, 1959, 1962, 1967,* Parts 1, 2, & 3, Washington, D.C., Maryland, and Virginia; U.S. Civil Service Commission, *Annual Report of Federal Civilian Employment in the United States by Geographical Area, 1967.*

Table 1-2

**Projected Labor Force, 1970-2000, for the
Washington, D.C. Metropolitan Area (In Thousands)**

Employment	1970		1980		1990		2000	
	Number	Percent	Number	Percent	Number	Percent	Number	Percent
Total	1,120	100.0	1,404	100.0	1,745	100.0	2,122	100.0
Federal	389	35.0	477	33.2	558	32.0	653	30.8
Private	731	65.0	957	66.8	1,187	68.0	1,469	69.2
Manufacturing	75	6.8	107	7.5	139	8.0	178	8.4
Construction	68	6.1	75	5.9	102	5.8	121	5.7
Wholesale/Retail	189	17.0	245	17.1	293	16.9	350	16.5
F.I.R.E.	61	5.4	81	5.6	97	5.6	116	5.4
Transportation/ Utilities	63	5.6	73	5.1	88	5.0	105	4.9
Services	242	22.6	326	22.8	419	23.9	537	25.2
Other	33	2.9	40	4.3	49	2.8	62	2.9

Source: U.S. National Capital Regional Planning Council, *Regional Development Guide,*
1966-2000 (Washington, D.C.: U.S. National Capital Planning Commission, 1966).

growth in automobile ownership, the building of Route 495, a circumferential highway around Washington, D.C., and improved communication techniques might encourage employment decentralization.

If Washington, D.C.'s service-based private sector continues to decentralize as the population becomes more and more suburban, then the key to the city's future as a place of employment seems to lie in future locational decisions made by the federal government. If future estimates of the National Capital Planning Commission (NCPC) and past trends are indicators, then the city should retain approximately 60 percent of all federal employment in the region through the year 1990.

The federal presence will continue to attract business and trade associations, consultants, research organizations, and other kinds of professional activity, thus emphasizing the city's position as a white collar, professional service city.

Recently however, there has been some indication that Washington, D.C. may not maintain its federal employment dominance. The Navy Department has just moved its 12,500 employees to several northern Virginia locations. Health, Education and Welfare, the second largest cabinet level department (in numbers of employees), has moved 6,000 employees from the District of Columbia to the Parkington Building in Rockville, Maryland. The Government Printing Office, employing 7,800 people, many of whom are non-white, low income workers, has announced plans to move its entire operation from downtown Washington, D.C., to Prince Georges County, Maryland. The Commerce Department and General Services Administration have moved workers to Crystal City in Arlington County, joining several other Federal agencies already there; and the Army is moving a unit to Charlottesville, Virginia.[14]

If these moves continue, and a report that the government is looking for still more office space in northern Virginia indicates that they will,[15] the District of Columbia may well begin to lose its position of dominance as the center of federal employment in the metropolitan area.

The exodus to the suburbs is increasingly isolating the city as a black core of poverty surrounded by white affluence. The District of Columbia Advisory Committee of the U.S. Commission on Civil Rights was recently told that the lack of housing for low income blacks in the suburbs is resulting in the District's being assigned the function of racial ghetto, low income housing source, and substandard employer.[16] As jobs move out, and middle class technical and professional families, both white and black, move out to follow their jobs, the city is left more and more to the poor, who are predominately black.[17]

**City and Suburb: The Extent
of Decentralization**

Data in Table 1-3 reveal two related employment trends in the region: the rapid growth of jobs in the suburbs, and some decline in the dominance of the city. Between 1954 and 1967, Washington, D.C.'s share of regional jobs fell from 71.8 percent to 56.6 percent, despite an absolute growth of 142,000 jobs. Looking at private and public sector employment separately, government jobs declined to a lesser degree than did jobs in private enterprise. The city's share of federal jobs declined by less than 6 percent to 66.8 percent of all federal jobs in the region, while its share of private sector employment declined by almost 14 percent to 51.4 percent. The decline in dominance of the central city has been in terms of the District's share of regional jobs. In no case, has the decentralization resulted in an absolute decline in jobs as was the case for New York[18] or for the cities surveyed by Kain.[19]

In view of the professional nature of much of the region's employment, the growth rates of the various categories take on added significance.

Table 1-3

Employment Growth and Change in Washington, D.C. and Its Suburbs, 1954-1967, (In Thousands) as a Percent of Regional Employment

Employment	1954 City No.	%	Suburb No.	%	1958 City No.	%	Suburb No.	%	1963 City No.	%	Suburb No.	%	1967 City No.	%	Suburb No.	%
Total	372	71.8	147	28.2	408	65.4	215	34.6	455	61.8	281	38.2	514	56.8	391	43.2
Federal	164	72.6	62	27.4	163	72.3	65	27.7	184	70.0	79	30.0	208	66.8	102	33.2
Private	208	71.2	84	28.8	245	61.9	151	38.1	271	54.9	202	45.1	306	51.4	289	48.6
Manufacturing	21	70.0	10	30.0	21	60.0	14	40.0	22	44.0	28	56.0	23	47.0	26	53.0
Wholesale	17	85.0	3	15.0	18	78.3	5	21.7	19	63.3	11	36.7	19	52.8	17	47.2
Retail	54	67.5	26	32.5	55	59.2	38	40.8	60	48.4	64	51.6	59	40.6	86	59.4
Construction	19	54.4	16	45.6	21	45.7	25	54.3	22	45.8	26	54.2	23	37.1	39	62.9
Transportation/Utilities	22	70.9	9	29.1	25	64.1	14	35.9	24	64.9	13	35.1	29	58.0	21	42.0
F.I.R.E.	27	82.4	7	17.6	28	71.9	11	28.1	28	65.2	15	34.8	36	59.0	25	41.0
Services	48	78.7	13	21.3	77	69.4	34	30.6	95	67.4	46	32.6	118	61.9	73	38.1

Source: Table 1-2 above.

The two categories that might logically be expected to have the largest number of white collar or professional employees—finance, insurance, real estate, and professional services—experienced the largest absolute growth. At the other extreme were the blue collar, semiskilled positions in manufacturing, wholesale and retail trade. Jobs in these categories experienced the smallest growth in both absolute and percentage terms.

Despite a quantitative increase of 40,000 jobs between 1954 and 1967, government employment in the suburbs now accounts for a smaller proportion of total employment than it did in 1954. Thus while the suburbs have increased their share of federal jobs by almost 7 percent to 33.2 percent, such jobs accounted for less of the total suburban labor force in 1967 than they did in 1954.

Qualitatively, employment growth in the suburbs has not differed greatly from change in the District. Services, the only category to increase its share of the city market, was the largest single gainer in the suburbs. Interestingly enough, the District's growth of 10 percent surpassed the northern Virginia growth of 9.3 percent and was only one percentage point behind the 11.2 percent growth of the Maryland suburbs.

The data presented in Table 1-4 show the absolute change in jobs between 1954 and 1967 for the central city and suburbs. During this period, the suburbs had an increase of almost 104,000 jobs more than the city. Washington, D.C. managed to outdistance its suburbs in only two categories, government and services. In the other six job listings, absolute suburban growth far surpassed that of the city. These data show most clearly the shift from central city dominance of the employment market to a more balanced regional distribution of jobs. Almost two-thirds of all new jobs in the region were located in the suburbs, not in the city.

At the same time, the growth that is taking place within the city is largely in office and white-collar types of occupations, with all other kinds of jobs showing a marked preference for the suburbs. These findings have implications not only for the kind of economic base that will support the city in the year 2000, but also for the ability of central city residents to get, keep, or change jobs, especially in industrial, commercial, or other non-white-collar occupations.

Paralleling the decentralization of jobs has been a decrease in the use of public transportation facilities. One expert attributes this to a reduction in the number of people requiring service into and out of the city during morning and evening rush hours.[20] Since 1940, the transit industry has lost almost four billion revenue passengers. Meanwhile, the number of routes served by commuter railroads has declined with remaining service becoming less frequent and less attractive.[21]

Equipment on the typical public transit route is likely to be old, dirty, not

Table 1-4

**Employment Change for the District of Columbia and Its
Suburbs, 1954-1967, in Absolute Terms (In Thousands)**

Employment	District of Columbia	Suburbs
Total	141	246
Federal	43	37
Private	98	206
Manufacturing	2	17
Wholesale	2	14
Retail	4	60
Construction	4	23
Transportation/ Utilities	7	12
F.I.R.E.	9	19
Services	70	66

Source: Table 1-3 above. Figures represent absolute numerical growth in jobs from 1954 to 1967.

air-conditioned, and generally in need of replacement. Trains are as likely to be late as not, while buses may skip stops to make up lost time, or may not even come at all.

Except for the seven metropolitan areas that have a rail rapid transit system,[f] practically all metropolitan areas depend entirely on their street systems to accommodate the movement of people. As has been pointed out in almost all of the literature on the commuter problem or the urban crisis, the problem is essentially one of public transit designed for the city of 1900 trying to serve the metropolitan area of 1970. Since the basic transportation systems of most urban areas were established, such areas have grown in population, undergone significant changes in land use and in the location of people and industry, and have grown in physical size as well.

Between 1940 and 1960, the population of urban areas grew from 78 million to 125 million. In many of these areas (especially the larger ones) this growth

[f]New York, Chicago, Cleveland, Philadelphia, Boston, and the systems under construction in San Francisco and Washington, D.C.

took place entirely on the fringes of the area with the central city experiencing little growth if not declining in absolute terms. Within this aggregate shift lies a complex pattern of population movement which has helped to intensify the commuting problem. In the large older urban areas, a significant portion of the population has abandoned the city for the suburbs. At the same time, large numbers of unskilled, rural, non-white people have migrated to the city. The result of these movements has been that between 1950 and 1966, the non-white population of central cities has almost doubled while the white population has decreased. In Washington, D.C., the non-white population has increased from 53.9 percent to 77 percent of the population, while whites in the city have declined from 46.1 percent to 23 percent during the period 1960 to 1969.[22]

A third trend can also be cited in the recent movements of urban area residents; they are moving from more dense to less dense housing. With more land being occupied, the average density of the entire metropolitan region is reduced.

Suburban development usually is low density as contrasted to medium or high density central city development. Obviously, the suburban development pattern requires more land per one-thousand population than does the city pattern. From 1920 to 1960, the average density of all urban areas in the United States decreased from 6,580 to 4,230 people per square mile. By 1980, the average density is expected to decrease by another 390 people per square mile to 3,840 people per square mile.[23]

For the commuter, this growth and dispersion has resulted in a longer trip to work. At this point, one conclusion seems certain: the task of urban transportation systems in the future will be to move more people over greater distances between where they are and where they want to go.

For the most part, urban mass transit systems have not developed in response to these changing needs and conditions. Routes have remained constant despite population shifts and land use changes. Central city transit systems often stop for no other valid reason than having reached the city's political boundaries. When transit routes were first established, few people lived outside of the city so there was no need to extend service beyond the city limits.

As suburbs grew, transit charters and legal restraints limited transit expansion that could have responded to the new growth. What in essence has happened is that traditional urban mass transit systems established to serve the downtown oriented city of the 1900's have not changed despite the growth and decentralization of people and jobs in the modern metropolitan area.

Today less than one-third of all workers live and work outside of the central city. By 1985, however, according to one expert, one-half of all workers will live and work outside the city.[24] In addition, there will be a significant number of reverse commuters—people living in the central city but working in the suburbs.

Almost all of the increase in travel will be by automobile. Public transit trips will gain only marginally from the changing travel patterns (from downtown oriented to radial or reverse trips) because of the preference for automobile travel.[25]

According to the 1960 Census, two-thirds of all employed persons living in metropolitan areas traveled to work in automobiles while only 19 percent used public transportation. It is estimated that in every metropolitan area more than 75 percent of all trips are made by car, with 90 percent or more the figure in some areas.[26]

Public Policy Implications

Ironically, metropolitan transportation systems too often leave unserved those who most need service: the poor, the handicapped, the old, and the young. Typically, the poorer people are, the more they are dependent upon public transportation to get around the metropolis. Automobile ownership statistics document this situation dramatically. In 1967, 75 percent of those households with an annual income under $1,000 owned no car; in the $1,000-1,999 group, the figure was 62 percent; it was 47 percent in the $2,000-2,999 category; while only 5 percent of all families in the $10,000-14,999 category had no car.[27]

If a man cannot afford an automobile, and public transit does not go where he needs to go or wants to go, if his job (or one he is qualified for) is in the suburbs, and if racial and economic discrimination in housing prevents him from moving closer to his job, then that man is effectively constrained from earning a living.

As more central business district jobs become white collar, and an increasing proportion of unskilled and semiskilled jobs leave the city, poor people are more disadvantaged than ever by public transportation systems that focus on central business districts and stop at city limits.[28]

Nearly one-third of the urban population suffers serious disadvantages from being inadequately or not served by the vast auto-based transportation systems on which we have come to depend. To quote Alan Altshuler:

... in the course of opting for an automobile civilization, which provides unprecedented mobility for those who can take full advantage of it, the national majority has chosen to ignore the problems this civilization creates for those who cannot. . . .

At a time when the central issue of American domestic politics is equality, public policy has massively reinforced the tendency of consumer choice (in favor of the automobile) to open up an ever wider "mobility gap" between those who have and those who lack access to a car.[29]

These are the "captives" left to use public transit or go without transportation. If transit service continues to deteriorate or be eliminated, many of these carless households will be relegated to a more isolated and narrow world, while automobile owners around them will enjoy the benefits of a society that caters to the car.

If society were willing or able to provide for the overnight redistribution of the entire population so that the mobility problems presented above would disappear, there would be no need to search for short range programs. As we noted earlier however, housing market discrimination will continue for some time,[30] so short run solutions to long range problems must be sought. If so-called "ghetto-gilding"[31] approaches are unacceptable on both moral and economic grounds, and if the ghetto leads to the social disintegration of its residents,[32] then, social scientists are beginning to ask, why not invest in transit systems to take ghetto residents to jobs, shopping, medical care, and other urban public services.[33]

From the policy perspective, a major problem is that too little is known about the desired mobility of the inner city resident.

What evidence exists is based on highway planning and land use studies, and these have dealt with the average behavior of a resident within a census tract or traffic zone. To date, urban transportation research has failed to consider the mobility characteristics of differing groups of people in any comprehensive sense.[34] In addition, our knowledge of the priority that the poor accord their own immobility is extremely limited—nor do we know anything about the degree to which the poor would act differently if specific kinds of efforts were made to relieve their mobility problems.[35] If we knew the mobility preferences of the poor, it *might* be relatively simple to design public policy to achieve these preferences and correct present imbalances. Because that knowledge is lacking, urban mass transit decisions have acted to subsidize middle income families with transit systems designed to serve downtown and other white collar areas more often than industrial ones.

Martin Wohl has argued that rapid transit systems as typically designed:

... tend to serve a small minority of higher-income suburbanites rather than the bulk of even downtown—much less urban—workers. ... Almost all downtown workers and about 75 percent of workers in the central city of a metropolis live within that central city; only a few downtown and central city workers—mainly upper- or middle-income people—live in suburbs. As a consequence, most new rapid transit is aimed principally at a small portion of our urban travelers—those downtown workers who live in the suburbs.[36]

Although public policy is largely responsive to the known preferences and values of specific interests, the most vocal, articulate, and self-selected urban spokesmen have come from the middle or upper classes. The programs they have supported and succeeded in effectuating have not been advanced in their own self-interest, but have been advanced under the assumption that all people hold (or ought to hold) the same goals they do.[37]

Since the McCone Commission Report, the transit needs of inner city residents have received wide attention, and because public policy is more responsive to expressed needs than to unknown needs, we might logically expect that inner city needs have received some policy attention. However, actual planning for such needs may not reflect such an awareness. Banfield has argued that in an innovative situation, a planner will:

(1) minimize the importance of problematic or intangible elements (the adoption of a system of free transit or subsidized automobile ownership for poor people);
(2) support solutions which have basis in fact and underrate those that require subjective judgments or reliance on unknown probabilities;
(3) support solutions on which there is general agreement while minimizing those that are controversial or unconventional;
(4) favor quantifiable solutions while underrating intangible and indefinite approaches (favoring cost-benefit measures while ignoring "quality of life" problems).[38]

Transportation thus becomes an area for testing the ability of public policy machinery in the United States to respond to the recently expressed needs of urban minorities. With increasing pressure on policy makers and governmental leaders for improved public transportation, a basic policy question to be asked (and answered) is how well the travel requirements of different groups are being met and why. It would seem that if the proposed subway system in Washington, D.C. (and other cities) seeks to serve all the people, an explicit effort has to be made to determine the travel requirements of different groups of potential users.

Plan of the Research Presentation

The following chapter will provide an analysis of the current transportation system of the National Capital region, and the anticipated impact of METRO.[g] Particular attention will be given to the travel needs of inner city residents. For this reason, the chapter will also include survey data on residents of four Washington, D.C. inner city neighborhoods relevant to their transportation needs and preferences. The specific objective in using survey data from the District of Columbia will be to investigate the degree to which inner city residents are

[g]The official name for the rail rapid transit system under construction in the National Capital area.

dependent upon some means of transportation other than the privately owned automobile, and the extent to which the present and proposed systems of public transportation fit the mobility needs of this population. Needs will be defined on the basis of attitudinal data as well as on calculations of employment opportunities in relation to the place of residence.

The survey data employed are part of a 1968 home interview and mail-in survey of the Washington, D.C. metropolitan area conducted by the Metropolitan Washington Council of Governments (Wash.-COG). The sample used in the survey was a 3.5 percent sample of all the households in the Washington, D.C. metropolitan area, yielding a sample size of approximately 29,000 household units. Within a household each individual over the age of five[h] who traveled on a specific day[i] was interviewed. For the four neighborhoods used in this research, a total of 246 interviews were recorded.

The demographic characteristics of the residents of the study areas will be fully explored in the following chapter. At this point it is sufficient to point out that most are black, very few meet the technical standard of poverty, and a significant minority are without automobiles.

Following the transportation analysis, two chapters on the evolution of METRO will be presented. An integral part of these chapters is a series of evaluations on the nature of the decision-making process for METRO and resulting constraints and limitations on the final form of the system as they affect the travel needs and requirements of inner city residents. The major objective of these chapters is to analyze as fully as possible the way in which decisions at one point in time affected later developments, and how by making certain service and policy decisions, future options were foreclosed. As will be indicated in later chapters, some early decisions limited the extent to which the proposed transit system could be adopted to the travel needs of inner city residents.

In the development of the METRO system value choices were made. The concluding chapter attempts to make these choices explicit, to show what they were, how they evolved, and their implications for the study of public policy. The final chapter will also fit planning, decision-making, and service into an overall framework in order to analyze some of the value consequences of the transportation planning process in the Nation's Capital.

---

[h]Children under the age of five were not assumed to be able to make independent trips and thus were not included in the sample design.

[i]Interviewers were given three days past a defined "travel date" to complete an interview. Travel dates were randomly distributed throughout the workweek to assure an even representation of the entire workweek.

2

Transportation in the Region

For the most part, the commuter's journey to work is by automobile or carpool. Of the 6.5 million suburban residents working in central cities in 1960, 80.4 percent traveled to work in private transportation, while only 15 percent used public transportation.[a] For central city residents working in the city, 29.7 percent used public transportation while 56.9 percent relied on private means of transportation to get to work.[b] Finally, only 12.1 percent of central city residents working in the suburbs used public transportation to get to work. Table 2-1 presents data for all metropolitan areas over 100,000 population and for the Washington, D.C. metropolitan area as to place of work and mode of travel used.

The Washington, D.C. area in 1960 had a smaller percentage of city and a larger percentage of suburban residents working in the central city than the other metropolitan areas in the country, and had more city residents commuting to the suburbs than the national average.

Reliance on public transportation to get to work was also greater in the National Capital area than in the other SMSA's. City and suburban residents, regardless of their place of work, used public transit more in the Washington, D.C. area than in the rest of the nation's metropolitan areas.

Who Uses Public Transportation

Public transit usage has been shown to decline as the distance of the work place from the central business district increases, with higher personal income, and with higher occupational status.[1] Thus, given a choice of travel modes, a person will be less likely to patronize public transit if: (1) he lives or works a long distance from downtown, (2) he has a high income, and (3) his occupation is professional or white-collar. Conversely, low income, blue-collar, or semiskilled workers living or working in the city would be expected to use public

---

[a]The remaining 4.6 percent walked to work, worked at home, or did not report their mode of travel.

[b]The remaining 13.4 percent walked to work, worked at home, or did not report their mode of travel.

Table 2-1

Place of Work and Workers Using Public Transportation for SMSA's Over 100,000 Population and Washington, D.C., 1960

	Live in Central City				Live in Suburbs			
	Work in City		Work in Suburbs		Work in City		Work in Suburbs	
	Number (000)	Per-cent	Number (000)	Per-cent	Number (000)	Per-cent	Number (000)	Per-cent
Place of Work[a]								
SMSA's	18,300	82.7	2,000	9.2	6,500	33.0	11,300	57.7
Washington,								
D.C. area	269	78.3	36	10.2	213	43.9	237	48.9
Workers Using Public								
Transportation								
SMSA's		29.7		12.1		15.0		4.6
Washington,								
D.C. area		43.3		32.2		18.4		5.8

[a]Place of work percentages do not total 100 percent because of those residents who work outside of the SMSA of residence.

Source: U.S. Department of Commerce, Bureau of the Census, *Census of Population: 1960, Supplementary Reports, Place of Work and Means of Transportation to Work: 1960.*

transportation more than their suburban counterparts. Table 2-2 presents the supporting data for these expectations.

The data show that in no case is public transit used by a plurality of professional workers regardless of their place of residence. Similarly, in all cases but one, the public transit group earns less than the group relying on the automobile to get to work. The one case that does not fit the pattern is that of the white suburban commuter, the stereotype commuter.

Who Uses A Car

If we omit the very poor, the assumed universality of automobile ownership in the United States is almost a reality. In 1967, 78 percent of all American families owned one or more automobiles, while only 22 percent of all families had no automobile. Ownership, however, varies significantly with income. In

Table 2-2
Journey to Work of City and Suburban Residents: 1960,
for the Washington, D.C. SMSA (In Thousands)

	Live in City Work in				Live in Suburbs Work in			
	City[a]		Suburbs[b]		City[c]		Suburbs[d]	
	Num- ber	Per- cent	Num- ber	Per- cent	Num- ber	Per- cent	Num- ber	Per- cent
Total	270	100	37	100	213	100	238	100
Public	115	42.5	12	31.4	38	17.9	14	5.7
Race White	52	45.2	3	21.7	37	96.4	11	80.1
Non-white	63	54.8	9	78.3	1	3.6	3	19.9
Occupation Professional	16	14.1	1	7.7	11	30.6	1	8.3
White-collar	42	36.9	2	15.9	20	54.5	6	50.0
Other	77	49.0	9	76.4	6	14.9	5	41.7
Income $1-3,000	70	62.9	9	79.6	14	37.6	9	72.4
$4-9,999	39	34.8	2	19.8	19	50.7	3	24.8
$10,000-+	3	2.3	—	.6	4	11.7	—	2.8
Private	106	39.3	24	65.1	170	79.9	173	72.8
Race White	60	57.5	12	48.4	166	97.7	163	94.3
Non-white	46	42.5	12	51.6	4	2.3	10	5.7
Occupation Professional	30	29.3	6	26.9	64	40.9	55	34.0
White-collar	34	33.6	5	23.4	52	32.7	47	28.8
Other	38	37.1	11	49.7	42	26.4	59	37.2
Income $1-3,999	37	35.7	10	43.1	30	19.0	67	39.6
$4-9,999	58	55.0	12	52.2	104	61.0	86	50.9
$10,000 +	9	9.3	1	4.7	35	20.0	16	9.5

[a]Excludes 6,111 taxi users, 30,305 who walk to work, 7,858 who work at home, and 4,426 not reported.

[b]Excludes 150 taxi users, 236 who walk to work, and 756 not reported.

[c]Excludes 666 railroad users, 852 taxi users, 466 who walk to work, and 2,502 not reported.

[d]Excludes 55 railroad users, 1,045 taxi users, 25,541 who walk to work, 16,241 who work at home, and 7,303 not reported.

Source: U.S. Department of Commerce, Bureau of the Census, *Census of Population: 1960*, Vol. 2, *Journey to Work*, Table 2.

1967, 75 percent of those families with an annual income under $1,000 had no automobile, while at the $2,000-3,000 level, 47 percent had no car. At the other extreme, once an annual income of $7,500 or more is reached, between 93 percent and 94 percent of all families own at least one automobile.[2]

For Washington, D.C. in 1960, 47.3 percent of all families, at all income levels, had no automobile, while carless families in the suburbs were only 8.6 percent of all suburban families. By 1969, the percentage of carless families in the District of Columbia had fallen to 40 percent of the population.[3]

From Table 2-2 we see that automobile users are mainly white suburban residents earning between $4,000 and $10,000 annually. The white Washington, D.C. resident is more likely to use an automobile than public transit to get to work, regardless of his place of employment. The same is true for his suburban counterpart, but to a greater degree. For the non-white central city resident the choice is public transit, except where the work place is in the suburbs. In this case, we find 3,000 more non-white commuters using cars than buses in their suburban work trip. Given the difference in occupational and income characteristics between the two non-white groups, it is quite likely that the non-white reverse commuter who uses a bus to get to work cannot afford an automobile. Table 2-2 shows that almost 80 percent of the non-white reverse commuters earned $4,000 or less in 1960, while only 43.1 percent of their auto-using neighbors were in the same income bracket.

In occupation terms, less than 25 percent of the bus riding non-white reverse commuters held professional or white-collar jobs while fully half of the auto using group did.

METRO: Tomorrow's Transportation in the National Capital Region

As will be pointed out in the next chapter, much of the planning done in the early stages of the subway program was predicated upon the continued dominance of the central city and CBD of the region's economic base. The employment trends discussed earlier indicate that the District will continue to be the largest single employment site in the region, but that its relative dominance will decline.

In trying to determine the quality of service METRO will provide to various groups, several complex and sometimes contradictory factors must be considered. The Washington Metropolitan Area Transit Authority (WMATA) has acknowledged the existence of such factors and has pointed out that the construction of METRO and rising downtown parking rates will tend to increase transit usage; while increasing automobile ownership, the continued suburbanization of people and jobs, and continued freeway construction in the region all will have a negative impact on transit use.[4]

A number of studies[5] have analyzed the price elasticity for different modes and between different modes of transportation. In all cases, the price of public transportation is not elastic. This means that little abandoning of the automobile for public transit should be expected as a result of fare decreases on public transit systems.

Other factors that may have a negative effect on public transit use are an increase in family income, an increase in automobile ownership, declining central city population combined with rising suburban population, declining central city and increasing suburban employment, and increased urban sprawl.[6]

Even considering these constraints on transit usage, WMATA has estimated that METRO will serve between 49 percent and 72 percent of all CBD oriented trips during the average morning rush hours in the year 1990.

The data in Table 2-3 are expected, and at the same time somewhat surprising. While the downtown patronage figures provide no surprises, the small proportion of riders using METRO to reach non-CBD central city locations is somewhat unexpected. An examination of the city portion of the system (see Figure 4-10, page 91) shows that areas outside downtown will just not be served as well as the CBD. Georgetown, the Wisconsin Avenue corridor, most of southeast Washington, D.C., and the upper Georgia Avenue corridor will not be served by METRO. People working in the non-CBD parts of the city then will have little incentive to use METRO since it will require an extremely long walk or a bus ride after leaving the subway station.

So, for the average individual, the work trip would consist of an auto or bus ride from home to the subway station, a rail trip to town, and then a bus, taxi ride, or long walk to the place of work. Transportation studies have long pointed out that once a commuter gets into his automobile, the battle to get him to use public transit is all but lost since he is extremely unlikely to leave his car at a parking lot and take a bus or rail vehicle.

The low utilization of METRO by suburban destined workers, regardless of their origin point (which is assumed to be their place of residence), points up the downtown oriented nature of the system. With Alexandria and Arlington excluded, maximum reverse use of the system is expected to be by District of Columbia residents working in Montgomery County. Even here, only 21 percent of those traveling from the city to that suburban Maryland county are expected to patronize METRO.[7] While suburban employment is growing both relatively and absolutely faster than city employment, few non-CBD trips will be made by METRO.

One reason is the nature of suburban employment. With few exceptions, it is characterized by low-density, dispersed job locations. When viewed from the

Table 2-3

Percent of 1990 Morning Peak Hour Work Trips Using Transit

Origin	Destination					
	CBD	Rest of District	Prince Georges	Mont-gomery	Fairfax	Alexandria/ Arlington
District of Columbia	72	26	10	21	14	42
Prince Georges County	53	13	2	9	6	24
Montgomery County	56	14	2	5	3	25
Fairfax County	49	11	2	6	1	17
Alexandria/Arlington	63	16	6	14	8	30

Source: WMATA, *Traffic Forecast*.

perspective of a potential rider who wishes to reach a suburban center, rail coverage is poor. There is little incentive for the auto-owning public to use any form of public transit to reach suburban work areas. Generally, traffic congestion is less at an outlying center than it is downtown, so the work trip is easier and more convenient. In addition, parking at a suburban center is either free or much less expensive than downtown.[8]

The Alexandria and Arlington figures are high in comparison to the rest of the suburban jurisdictions simply because of the employment concentration located between Rosslyn and National Airport in northern Virginia. One of the METRO lines will serve over 10,000 relocated Navy Department employees at Parkington and more than 11,000 office and white-collar workers in the Rosslyn complex. The line serving the Pentagon, Crystal City, and National Airport will serve more than 50,000 workers.[9]

Of primary importance in the ability of METRO to produce its expected annual patronage of 292.6 million in the year 1990 is what happens to the current system of public transportation in the region, the bus system. WMATA has estimated that upwards of 70 percent of all METRO riders will reach the train station by bus.[10] The Voorhees staff in a 1967 future patronage study, forecast that 65.5 percent of all peak hour riders would use a bus to get to the subway station.[11] An estimate of the number of trips involving a double bus transfer was separately prepared. These are trips that require bus travel at both ends of the rail trip. A total of 15.9 percent of all trips during an average twenty-four hour period were estimated to require two bus rides. It was further estimated that 80.7 percent of all METRO trips would require a bus transfer at either or both ends of the rail trip.[12]

These estimates are based on some rather significant assumptions. First, the present bus system was assumed to be coordinated with the rail service.

If such redirection of the bus lines was not accomplished, ". . . but instead . . . operated in inefficient competition with the rail lines, the number of persons transferring from bus to rail will be lower, and the total rail patronage will be correspondingly lower."[13]

A second major assumption of the Voorhees study was that of free transfer privileges between rail and bus. If a charge for transferring is established, Voorhees concluded that overall patronage would decline. Finally, if downtown employment did not increase as projected, patronage to downtown (the key to the success of the entire system) would be correspondingly lowered.[14]

How negative some of the above mentioned effects would be is a question that METRO officials will not publicly answer.[c] But even without specific data it is reasonable to assume that a rail system depending on buses for bringing 70 percent of its riders to the rail stations will be in serious trouble if the buses operate in competition with the subway.

The importance of the eventual use of the buses is also seen in that there will be only 30,100 parking spaces in the METRO system which hopes to serve 939,000 people daily.

The apparent solution to the bus problem lies in the public takeover of the bus companies in the region. In April, 1969, Senator Joseph Tydings (D-Md.) introduced legislation providing for the public ownership of D.C. Transit because ". . . an adequate mass transit bus system . . . cannot be provided at the present time at reasonable fares by the ordinary operation of private enterprise without public participation; . . ."[15]

The final resolution of what happens to the bus companies still appears to be some time in the future. Congress has shown no real desire to settle the matter and it might take a strike similar to the one in 1955 which led to the demise of D.C. Transit's predecessor, or a complete collapse of the company before Congress will act. Whether or not the issue needs to be solved in the immediate future is open to question. METRO officials are continuing with system planning and construction on the somewhat tacit assumption that they eventually will be the regional transit authority coordinating rail and bus travel.

On the other hand, the task of generating patronage once the system is built, and the even more immediate need to sell $880 million worth of revenue bonds

---

[c]During interviews with WMATA officials and Voorhees representatives this specific question was never adequately answered.

on the open market would be much easier if such crucial decisions were made now. In today's auto-dominated commuter picture METRO is attempting to do a unique thing: make rail rapid transit a financially sound and profitable operation. For this to be done, patronage affecting questions should be resolved as soon as possible with as little unpleasant publicity as possible.

Transportation and Employment:
Getting to Work in 1980

In trying to forecast residents, employment, and travel patterns for 1980, the growth trends of the 1950's and 1960's must be examined for their relevance for the 1970's.

The future work trip will take on differing characteristics depending on the degree to which the employment trends outlined in Chapter 1 are realized. As jobs and people are scattered throughout the region, the automobile will be relied on even more than at present for the journey to work, and may well become an almost exclusive mode of travel for the non-work trip.

Downtown jobs will be served by METRO from almost every populated part of the region while non-CBD jobs and suburban employment will receive much less comprehensive service. Based on the estimated patronage figures in Table 2-3, the future work trip should take on the characteristics in the following diagram:

Place of Work

Place of Residence	Downtown	Rest of District of Columbia	Suburbs
City	METRO/Bus	Bus/Auto	Auto
Suburbs	METRO/Auto	Auto	Auto

The analysis just completed has more or less assumed the existence of a homogeneous transportation public. That is, except for a few references to the reverse commuter and low automobile ownership among the poor, the preceding analysis has treated all people as having equal ability to choose an optimal mix of housing, employment, and travel choices. Our task is now to look at the previously forgotten group; the inner-city, low income resident who works in the suburbs: the reverse commuter.

The Reverse Commuter

The effort to present a comprehensive picture of the reverse commuter will focus on present transportation patterns, and so far as possible, desired or preferred patterns.

Route maps and schedules published by the D.C. Transit Company will be used to plot several "typical"[d] work trips for inner city residents to suburban job sites. The employment locations presented here were originally used by Development Research Associates in calculating the accessibility of the disadvantaged to employment sites using METRO.[16] In addition, the areas chosen represent the largest Federal, commercial, and industrial areas in the Maryland suburbs. Origin points within the four neighborhoods chosen were assumed to be the intersection of two streets and were randomly selected from all such possible origin points. The reader should note that all travel time reported is time spent on a bus and does not include walking to the bus stop, waiting between buses, or walking to a destination.

Walking time can be estimated using the accepted transportation criterion of one-quarter mile as the maximum.

Waiting time for a bus is usually calculated as one-half the time between the arrival of two buses because all patrons are assumed to arrive at the bus stop in a random manner. Thus, if the time between the arrival of one bus and the arrival of a second bus is twenty minutes, a waiting time of ten minutes would be assigned to that portion of the trip because of the random arrival assumption.

The effort to discover the desired travel patterns of inner city respondents has several goals, the most important of which is to provide a detailed description and analysis of the subjective transportation wants and policy preferences of inner city residents. This knowledge is important if we are to accurately measure the various inputs to the planning of the National Capital area's rail rapid transit system.

Originally the Suitland Federal Center and the Marlow Heights commercial center in southeastern Prince Georges County were included in the list of suburban employment sites to be analyzed here. It later became necessary to omit these areas because D.C. Transit does not serve them. Hence for a resident of the southeast Washington, D.C. area to reach relatively close suburban employment would require a bus ride to the District of Columbia-Maryland via D.C. Transit and then a transfer to a different company's vehicle, with no free transfer privileges between companies. For this individual then, the work trip would require at least two buses and two full fares.

---

[d]Because of the large number of trips originally involved, forty-eight, D.C. Transit's public information office would not check the writer's routes against their recommended system. Those that were checked were identical to the system's structure or differed only in where to transfer buses. In all cases the effort was made to get to work in the shortest amount of time possible using the fewest number of buses, not entirely compatible goals.

Table 2-4

Number of Buses, Number of Transfers, and Travel Time Between the Central City and Selected Suburban Job Sites for Washington, D.C. and Its Maryland Suburbs[a] (Number of Buses-Number of Transfers-Time)

Origins	Destinations					
	Prince Georges Plaza	Silver Spring	Wheaton	National Institutes of Health	National Bureau of Standards	Atomic Energy Commission
Northern Anacostia						
47th & Clay Sts. N.E.	3-2-:46	2-1-1:03	3-2-1:15	3-2-1:23	4-3-2:03	3-2-1:54
29th & O Sts. S.E.	3-2-:32	2-1- :58	3-2-1:10	2-1-1:23	3-2-2:03	2-1-2:28
Southern Anacostia						
15th & U Sts. S.E.	2-1-:39	2-1- :42	3-2- :54	3-2-1:23	3-2-1:20	3-2-1:52
4th & Nichols Sts. S.E.	3-2-:36	3-2-1:05	4-3-1:17	4-3-1:17	5-4-1:57	4-3-1:53
Central City						
Columbia & Sherman Rds. N.W.	3-2-:55	1-0- :18	2-1- :30	2-1- :45	3-2-1:10	2-1-1:12
Florida & Georgia Aves. N.W.	2-1-:37	1-0- :25	2-1- :37	2-1- :50	3-2-1:17	3-2-1:32
Catholic Univ.-Ft. Lincoln						
22nd & Monroe Sts. N.E.	2-1-:24	2-1- :47	3-2- :59	1-0-1:15	4-3-1:38	2-1-1:40
N. Capitol & Riggs Rd. N.E.	3-2-:46	2-1- :18	3-2- :30	1-0- :42	4-3-1:10	2-1-1:18

[a]Based on information gathered from D.C. Transit Company route maps and schedules.

For all neighborhoods the longest trips are to the National Bureau of Standards (NBS) in Gaithersburg and the Atomic Energy Commission (AEC) in Germantown. This is because they are twenty-five or more miles from the District, resulting in an extremely long ride, even on an express bus. Of the forty-three trips plotted, almost 54 percent (twenty-three) require more than one hour to complete with the same number (but not necessarily the same trips) requiring two or more buses. The Quayle study reported earlier supports this finding as 52 percent of those using two or more buses needed more than forty-five minutes to get to work.[17]

By neighborhood, the two areas east of the Anacostia River—areas geographically removed from the rest of the city—have the highest travel times and require the most number of transfers for all trips of the four neighborhoods studied. Again, this is a function of their distance from the central city and the suburban employment sites examined. It does however, pose a serious problem for the Anacostia area resident who must rely on public transit to get to work in the suburbs.

From southern Anacostia (4th and Nichols Streets S.E.) it takes an average of four buses and eighty-four minutes to get to work, not counting walking or waiting times. To the close-in suburb of Silver Spring, it takes three buses and sixty-five minutes to get to work. Thus, a southeast Washington, D.C. resident who can spend no more than one hour going to work cannot seriously consider Montgomery County as a possible job site.

Work trip conditions are noticeably better in the center city. All suburban job sites except the National Bureau of Standards and the Atomic Energy Commission are within a one hour's bus ride from the center city, and only the trip from Columbia and Sherman Roads N.W. to Prince Georges Plaza requires more than one bus transfer.

The bus line running to Silver Spring goes out Georgia Avenue, a major travel corridor for central city and suburban residents. As a result, almost any work place within walking distance of Georgia Avenue between downtown Washington, D.C. and Silver Spring is easily reached by bus. Similarly, the trip to the Wheaton regional commercial center can be accomplished with only one bus transfer, at the District of Columbia boundary. Thus, employment located between the District's boundary and Wheaton, Maryland (including Holy Cross Hospital) is accessible to residents of the central city. For these reasons too, the trip to the Atomic Energy Commission and the National Bureau of Standards can be made in less than one and one-half hours.

Residents of the Catholic University-Fort Lincoln area are in much the same position as central city residents. From the two origin points within the area, over half of the suburban destinations tested are less than one hour away by bus. Eliminating the Atomic Energy Commission and National Bureau of Standards sites, seven of the remaining eight suburban destinations are within an hour's bus ride from the area. It is interesting to note that the Catholic University-Fort Lincoln area, because of its high automobile ownership rate (see Table 2-5) and relatively central location, "needs" public transportation less than any of the other areas surveyed, but has as good or better service than any other area tested.

The full impact of the situation is visible in a special test performed by a reporter from the *Washington Post* in 1967. Starting from 31st Street and Alabama Avenue S.E. (between and to the east of the 15th and U Streets S.E. and 29th and O Streets S.E. locations used in this research) it took two hours and four buses to reach Chevy Chase, Maryland, just over the district line.[18] On rainy days and in other types of inclement weather, regular bus riders report their travel times increasing by as much as 50 percent.[19]

To put our travel times into a somewhat more realistic perspective, only 41 percent of the total time spent on a bus is spent in motion.[20] This figure assumes that a bus is operating in its "best" element—the no-transfer, downtown oriented trip.[21] Almost 13.5 percent of all bus travel time is spent walking to or from the bus, 20.9 percent is used up waiting for the bus to come, and traffic congestion and loading and unloading passengers consumes another 25 percent.[22]

In sharp contrast, almost 64 percent of auto travel time is spent in motion.[23] If the buses were able to increase their time in motion as a proportion of total travel time, more suburban jobs would become reachable within one hour, and buses would take on some of the advantages of automobile ownership.

Under present conditions, the long and intricate bus trips required to get to suburban job centers appears to be a major problem faced by inner city residents attempting to find work in the suburbs.

All travel times reported have been based on the assumption that the inner city worker works the "normal" nine-to-five work day. In other words, the schedules from which the travel times reported were taken were for vehicles operating during the morning peak hours (7 to 9 a.m.). As will be pointed out in the next chapter, a significant portion of travel to work from the ghetto is not during the peak demand period. Much of this type of travel occurs late at night or early in the morning when buses are operating much less frequently. What this of course means is the off-peak suburban workers face a more difficult and time consuming work trip than the population just described. In such a case, one might expect an individual to remain unemployed rather than face the vagaries of bus travel in off-peak hours. Bus service during off-peak hours, especially late at night, can be as infrequent as one bus every hour. An inner city resident having to travel to the suburbs in an off-peak period is truly a "captive" bus rider.[e]

---

[e]Normal transportation planning usage refers to a captive rider as one who has no option other than the bus, i.e., no automobile is available. It might refer to a carless household, or a suburban housewife whose husband takes the family car to work leaving her to ride the bus.

Table 2-5

Demographic Profile of Survey Area Respondents, by Area, by Percent[a]

	Area				
	District of Columbia[b]	Northern Anacostia	Southern Anacostia	Central City	Catholic Univ.-Ft. Lincoln
Sex					
Male	53.3	46.5	58.3	46.2	70.0
Female	46.7	53.5	41.7	53.7	30.0
Income					
$0-2,999	1.3	2.9	—	2.7	—
$3-5,999	23.1	34.3	19.6	28.0	—
$6-9,999	44.9	40.0	46.4	53.3	11.1
$10,000-+	30.7	22.9	34.0	16.0	88.9
Employed					
Yes	81.7	85.0	83.0	75.0	95.0
No	18.3	15.0	17.0	25.0	5.0
Occupation					
Professional, Technical, Managerial	20.7	28.9	16.9	18.6	30.0
Sales & Clerical	33.2	34.2	32.6	32.9	35.0
Skilled	10.6	7.9	10.1	11.4	15.0
Semi-skilled	13.4	13.2	14.6	11.4	15.0
Unskilled	4.1	2.6	3.4	7.1	—
Service	18.4	13.2	22.5	18.6	5.0
Employer					
Federal Gov't.	49.6	42.1	60.9	32.9	75.0
Manufacturing	2.2	—	2.2	2.6	5.0
Construction	6.6	2.6	6.5	7.9	10.0
Transportation/ Utilities	5.3	7.9	5.4	3.9	5.0
Wholesale/Retail	11.1	18.4	10.9	10.5	—
F.I.R.E.	3.5	2.6	—	9.2	—

(*continued*)

Table 2-5 (*Cont.*)

	Area				
	District of Columbia[b]	Northern Anacostia	Southern Anacostia	Central City	Catholic Univ.-Ft. Lincoln
Professional					
Services	12.8	21.1	9.8	14.5	5.0
Personal					
Services	8.8	5.3	4.3	18.4	—
Mode of Travel					
Car	37.4	41.9	37.9	28.7	60.0
Bus	41.9	44.2	43.7	45.0	15.0
Taxi/Train	.8	—	1.0	1.2	—
Auto Passenger	11.4	11.6	12.6	7.5	20.0
Number of Cars					
Available					
None	36.2	25.6	38.8	47.5	—
1	50.4	58.1	49.5	40.0	80.0
2	9.3	11.6	7.8	10.0	10.0
3	4.1	4.7	3.9	2.5	10.0
Race					
White	17.1	21.4	12.6	20.0	20.0
Non-white	82.9	78.6	87.4	80.0	80.0
Education					
Elementary	13.4	14.0	1.9	26.2	20.0
High School	61.8	48.8	74.8	52.5	60.0
College	24.8	37.2	23.3	21.2	20.0
Home Ownership					
Own	28.9	29.5	15.5	23.7	95.0
Rent	71.1	60.5	84.5	76.2	5.0

Sources:

[a]Metropolitan Washington Council of Governments, Transportation Planning Board, *Home Interview Survey*, (1968).

[b]Summary of the four neighborhoods investigated.

In view of the characteristics of the present bus system, our next task is to determine the subjective attitudes of inner city residents toward their present travel patterns, and how well they think METRO will serve their subjectively defined needs. Table 2-5 data provide a thumbnail sketch of survey area respondents. Men outnumber women simply because the survey was aimed at uncovering the travel attitudes of family heads and workers and did not try to replicate the exact sex distribution of the population in the survey areas. In addition, almost 83 percent of survey area respondents in the inner city are non-white.

In income terms, very few respondents fall into the Office of Economic Opportunity's (OEO) poverty class of $3,000 or less annual income. But at the same time, the OEO poverty definition is five years old and is probably outdated given inflation and changes in the standard of living. Relatively recent data indicate that it costs $10,503 a year to support a family of four in adequate but moderate living conditions in Washington, D.C.[24]

A low standard of living in the area for a family of four would be $6,907 annually while a high standard of living would require at least $15,350 annually.[25]

Baltimore, Maryland, less than forty miles from the Nation's Capital, ranks near the bottom of the list with $9,735 required to provide a moderate style of life for a family of four. These data indicate that the "poverty line" may be well above the $3,000 level although its exact location cannot be determined from the data. The Quayle survey cited earlier points out that at least one-half of all District of Columbia residents earning between $3,100 and $5,000 a year are living in poverty conditions.[26] By these criteria then, almost one-quarter of our respondents are living under poverty conditions. Using the $10,503 level, almost 70 percent of survey area respondents live less than a moderate style of life.

With the high cost of living in the Nation's Capital, it is not surprising that over 30 percent of the interviewees earn more than $10,000 annually. The Catholic University-Fort Lincoln area, which is "more suburban"[f] than the other three neighborhoods in the sample, is significantly oriented to a middle-class style of life.

The neighborhood findings are not out of line with the 1969 Quayle study of all adult District of Columbia residents. For the city as a whole, Quayle found one-third earning $5,000 a year or less, 41 percent earning between $5,100 and $10,000 a year, and 22 percent earning more than $10,000 annually.[27]

As to how people earn their money, the data indicate that almost half of them work for government at some level, be it Federal, state, local, police, or fire departments, or the military. Again, the "most suburban" neighborhood leads the others with three-fourths of its respondents working for the

---

[f]The data in Table 2-5 show that this area exhibits more of the popular characteristics of suburbia than do any of the other areas. Income, education, home ownership, and automobile ownership are higher here than in the other areas.

government. As was pointed out in our discussion of employment trends in the region, service jobs are the most important non-governmental category. Almost one-fourth of the interviewees are employed in the service industries, with over half of those involved in professional services.[g]

Personal service workers are, for the most part, concentrated in the central city. In this category we find parking lot attendants, barbers and beauticians, bowling alley employees, photographers, hotel and laundry workers, and others.

The high rate of personal service workers, 18.4 percent of the central city labor force, in the central city is realistic given the area's proximity to official and tourist Washington. We might normally expect to find a high concentration of people-serving industries in locations that attract tourists, government officials, lobbyists, convention goers, and meetings.

What is surprising is the relatively high proportion of professional, technical, and managerial workers reported in all the neighborhoods. For the four areas together, 20.7 percent of the respondents categorize themselves as professional, technical, or managerial. However, the 1960 Census reported that 21.8 percent of all Washington, D.C. residents were employed in one of these three categories. The national improvement in the employment status of blacks (over 80 percent of the survey respondents are non-white) is no doubt partially responsible for this rather high proportion of professional jobs. Between 1960 and 1967, non-whites in professional and technical jobs increased by 80 percent to 592,000 at the national level.[28] For managerial employees there was a 17 percent increase nationally to 209,000 such jobs for non-whites.[29]

Another contributing factor is the fact that Washington, D.C. is essentially a professional employment city. Hence, we might normally expect to find a concentration of such workers throughout the entire metropolitan area.[h]

Sales and clerical jobs total one-third of the work force in the survey area neighborhoods. Quayle, using slightly different definitions, reported that 32 percent of the city's work force was white-collar.[30] Blue-collar workers[i] comprise 46.5 percent of survey area employees. Although the statistics themselves are interesting, the trends they indicate are more important. Despite what we said about the District of Columbia's professional and service

---

[g]Professional service includes consulting work, medical, legal, and teaching services, non-profit organizations, charities, churches and schools, labor unions, research and development organizations, advertising agencies, writers, and others.

[h]It must be acknowledged that the survey data on which this analysis is based may be skewed in favor of higher income respondents. If this is so and the poor or low income residents of the four areas are under-represented in the survey, the conclusions drawn are all the more valid in terms of the transportation deprivation of the poor.

[i]Blue-collar has been created out of skilled, semiskilled, unskilled, and personal service categories.

orientation, respondents from the three inner city neighborhoods are blue-collar workers much more than they are professional or white-collar employees.

Furthermore, almost one respondent in five, 18.3 percent, was unemployed or did not work. This finding scales from a high of 25 percent in the central city to a low of 5 percent in the "suburban" neighborhood. This high level of unemployment is disturbing in itself, but the figures themselves do not reveal the entire picture. In discussing employment trends in the region, we pointed out that the economy of the Washington, D.C. area was tied to government, services, and retail trade. This has resulted in a relatively stable, high-wage employment pattern in which large scale or prolonged lay-offs or strikes are almost unheard of. It is thus reasonable to assume that those people who are out of work have been unemployed for some time and will probably remain jobless for some time in the future. Part of the reason is no doubt due to the region's professional orientation resulting in a relative scarcity (scarcity when compared to metropolitan areas of comparable size) of semiskilled, operative, or manufacturing kinds of jobs. But a lack of transportation to get to new and growing suburban job sites can also be cited as a contributing cause.[31]

In testifying before the Douglas Commission on urban problems, John Howard of the Washington, D.C. [NAACP] pointed out:

. . . we have jobs out in the suburbs. We are getting slow action on suburban housing [so] . . . we need some transportation to be able to get to the suburbs, because that is where all the building is going on. . . .

[Suburban jobs] are on the Beltway and places like that, but there's no transportation going out there. So you must be able to buy an automobile before you can go to work, and you know that is impossible.[32]

The Quayle survey points out that 48 percent of all Washington, D.C. residents drive to work or are in a carpool. But when the unemployed are controlled for, the automobile user group jumps to 60 percent of all city residents.[33] As might be expected, auto usage is closely tied to its availability. In the central city neighborhood having the lowest car use for work, automobile ownership is lowest; 47.5 percent of the respondents have no car at their disposal.

The Catholic University area has the highest proportion of auto usage for the work trip, and it also has the highest percentage of automobile availability. Northern Anacostia with one-half of its respondents using cars to get to work has almost three-fourths of those respondents having access to at least one car.

Home ownership data do not add much to the demographic pattern already developed. However, the data do point out that relatively few (28.9 percent) inner city respondents have been able to acquire one of the prerequisites of middle class status—ownership of a home. This finding helps to point out one of the differences between survey area residents and the rest of the city: 55 percent of all Washington, D.C. families own their own homes.[34]

METRO's ultimate success depends on a great many factors, not all of which are quantifiable or measurable at the present time. Some of the known factors are quality and frequency of service, comfort, reliability, and cost. But patronage is also related to one's satisfaction with his present work trip and how well (a subjective decision) METRO will fit the transportation requirements for getting to work.

We can anticipate that the greater the degree of satisfaction with one's present work trip the less likely he will be to abandon that pattern for METRO, or for anything else. Conversely, the less the satisfaction with the present work trip, the greater the tendency to patronize METRO.

Table 2-6

Satisfaction with Work Trip by Area, in Percent

Convenience	Northern Anacostia	Southern Anacostia	Central City	Catholic Univ.-Ft. Lincoln	Total
Very Convenient	20.9(9)	15.5(16)	17.5(14)	30.0(6)	18.3(45)
Convenient	44.2(19)	35.9(37)	46.2(37)	60.0(12)	42.7(105)
Inconvenient	23.3(10)	35.0(36)	20.0(16)	5.0(1)	25.6(63)
Very Inconvenient	7.0(3)	8.7(9)	10.0(8)	– –	8.1(20)
No Opinion	4.7(2)	4.9(5)	6.7(5)	5.0(1)	5.3(13)
Total	17.5(43)	41.9(103)	32.5(80)	8.1(20)	100.0(246)

Source: Metropolitan Washington Council of Governments, Transportation Planning Board, *Home Interview Survey* (Washington, 1968).

As Table 2-6 indicates, better than half of all respondents in each of the neighborhoods surveyed have favorable comments to make about their present work trip. Satisfaction is lowest in southern Anacostia, the neighborhood most geographically isolated from the rest of the city, while respondents in the Catholic University-Fort Lincoln area are well satisfied with the way they get to work. This rather favorable feeling towards transportation within these four neighborhoods shows that a majority of survey area respondents do not view transportation as a major or critical problem. Most are reasonably well satisfied although a large minority are critical of their present travel.

When satisfaction is measured by the specific kind of mode used to get to work, it becomes quite clear that the degree of satisfaction with the work trip is closely associated with the way people get to work. More than three-fourths of those who drive to work find their trip convenient or very convenient while only 42.8 percent of the bus riders make similar comments. By neighborhood, southern Anacostia respondents exhibit the highest dissatisfaction with present travel, with bus service receiving most of the critical comments. But even with auto users, over one-fifth find their work trip inconvenient or very inconvenient.

Table 2-7 also shows that 67.9 percent of all unfavorable comments about the present work trip come from bus riders while this group accounts for only 38.2 percent of all favorable comments. Automobile users are responsible for 49.9 percent of all favorable responses and only 20.9 percent of the unfavorable ones. These data further support the earlier conclusion that bus riders are considerably less satisfied with their present work trip than are people who drive to work.

The question now to be faced is how important present satisfaction and place of residence are in determining potential METRO use. It is reasonable to assume that dissatisfaction with one's present mode might lead to METRO utilization as a way to improve the work trip, and as we have just pointed out, bus users tend to be more dissatisfied than automobile users. If place of residence has any significance at all, residents of the Anacostia neighborhoods might be expected to patronize METRO than other respondents, all other things being equal.

As we progress from those who find their work trip very convenient to those who find it very inconvenient, anticipated METRO use increases steadily from 28.9 percent to 55 percent (see Table 2-8).

What is quite disturbing however, is the large proportion of survey area respondents who do not know if METRO will benefit them or not. Such a high proportion of uncertainty might be normal since completion of the entire regional system is still ten or so years away, although parts of the system are scheduled to be operating by 1972. But in view of the large scale public relations efforts to inform people of the system and its benefits, such uncertainty is not beneficial to the overall success of the system. This uncertainty is not unique to inner city residents. In his survey, Quayle found that 31 percent of all adult Washington, D.C. residents were not sure of their use of METRO (see Table 2-9).[35]

Because METRO, as designed, will serve downtown with greater frequency and more comprehensive service than the rest of the city or the suburbs, it seems relevant to inquire as to the work place of potential riders. The inquiry is not so much to discover the number of downtown versus suburban workers who will use METRO, but to determine if suburban workers feel that METRO will benefit them in their work trip.

As in our previous attempts to discover something about potential METRO patronage, Table 2-10 shows that over one-third of the central city workers and

Table 2-7

**Satisfaction with Work Trip by Mode and Area in Percent
and by Mode in Percent**

	Auto	Auto Passenger	Bus	Walk
		Northern Anacostia		
Very Convenient	38.9(7)	20.0(1)	— —	— —
Convenient	33.6(6)	40.0(2)	57.9(11)	— —
Inconvenient	22.4(4)	20.0(1)	26.3(5)	— —
Very Inconvenient	— —	20.0(1)	10.5(2)	— —
No Opinion	5.6(1)	— —	5.3(1)	— —
		Southern Anacostia		
Very Convenient	23.1(9)	23.1(3)	4.4(2)	— (2)
Convenient	51.3(20)	15.4(2)	26.7(12)	— —
Inconvenient	10.3(4)	53.8(7)	55.6(25)	— —
Very Inconvenient	12.8(5)	— —	8.9(4)	— —
No Opinion	2.6(1)	7.7(1)	4.4(2)	— —
		Central City		
Very Convenient	21.7(5)	— (2)	8.3(3)	— (4)
Convenient	56.5(13)	— (4)	38.9(14)	— (4)
Inconvenient	13.0(3)	— —	33.3(12)	— —
Very Inconvenient	4.3(1)	— —	16.7(6)	— —
No Opinion	4.3(1)	— —	2.8(1)	— —
		Catholic University-Fort Lincoln		
Very Convenient	25.0(3)	— (3)	— —	— —
Convenient	66.7(8)	— (1)	— (2)	— —
Inconvenient	— —	— —	— (1)	— —
Very Inconvenient	— —	— —	— —	— —
No Opinion	— —	— —	— —	— —

Table 2-7 (*Cont.*)

	Auto	Auto Passenger	Bus	Walk
	All Areas			
Very Convenient	26.1(24)	32.1(9)	4.9(5)	63.6(7)
Convenient	51.1(47)	32.1(9)	37.9(39)	36.4(4)
Inconvenient	12.0(11)	28.6(8)	41.7(43)	– –
Very Inconvenient	6.5(6)	3.6(1)	11.7(12)	– –
No Opinion	4.3(4)	3.6(1)	3.9(4)	– –

Source: Metropolitan Washington Council of Governments, Transportation Planning Board, *Home Interview Survey* (Washington, 1968).

almost one-half of the suburban workers do not know whether or not METRO will help them in their journey to work. It does not appear that lack of knowledge about the system is the reason for the uncertainty because only 6.4 percent of all respondents feel that they do not know enough about the system to commit themselves one way or the other. So a reason must be sought elsewhere. One possible explanation is that METRO is only one of several possible transportation improvements that can be accomplished, and not a very important one at that. In other words, freeways, buses, and better parking facilities might all be supported more by the general public than METRO.

As Table 2-11 indicates however, METRO is the most often mentioned transportation preference for the work trip, while commuter rail service ranks second. When the two rail solutions are combined, they account for 46.1 percent of all transportation preferences. Auto oriented solutions, including more freeways and better streets, are supported by less than 15 percent of the respondents. For non-work trips (trips that METRO planners refer to as "gravy" when forecasting patronage levels) METRO falls to third place as a transit solution while commuter rail service and better downtown parking facilities rank higher.

When people are asked to generalize about improving transportation in the downtown area and in the suburbs, METRO does not dominate the list of possible solutions. For downtown travel in general, commuter rail service again is preferred most by the respondents, while park and ride lots (to be explained shortly) ranked second. For suburban travel, METRO ranks second to providing better parking facilities and not far above commuter rail service as a possible improvement over present conditions.

Table 2-8

Expected METRO Utilization by Satisfaction with Present Journey to Work, in Percent

Will Use METRO	Rate Present Work Trip				
	Very Convenient	Convenient	Inconvenient	Very Inconvenient	Total
Yes	28.9(13)	33.3(35)	49.2(31)	55.0(11)	37.4(92)
No	44.4(20)	22.9(24)	9.5(6)	5.0(1)	20.7(51)
Don't Know	26.7(12)	42.9(45)	38.1(24)	40.0(8)	36.6(90)
No Opinion	– –	1.0(1)	3.2(2)	– –	5.3(13)
Total	18.3(45)	42.7(105)	25.6(63)	8.1(20)	100.0(246)

Source: Metropolitan Washington Council of Governments, Transportation Planning Board, *Home Interview Survey* (Washington, 1968).

Table 2-9

Expected METRO Utilization by Area, in Percent

Will Use METRO	Area				
	Northern Anacostia	Southern Anacostia	Central City	Catholic Univ.-Ft. Lincoln	Total
Yes	37.2(16)	43.7(45)	31.2(25)	30.0(6)	37.4(92)
No	23.3(10)	17.5(18)	20.0(16)	35.0(7)	20.7(51)
Don't Know	37.2(16)	33.0(34)	42.5(34)	30.0(6)	36.6(90)
No Opinion	2.3(1)	5.8(6)	6.2(5)	5.0(1)	5.3(13)
Total	17.5(43)	41.0(103)	32.5(80)	8.1(20)	100.0(246)

Source: Metropolitan Washington Council of Governments, Transportation Planning Board, *Home Interview Survey* (Washington, 1968).

Table 2-10
Expected METRO Use in Four Selected Neighborhoods by
Place of Work, in Percent

	Place of Work		
Will Use METRO	Washington, D.C.	Maryland Suburbs	Total
Yes	33.6(40)	31.8(7)	33.3(47)
No	25.2(30)	18.2(4)	24.1(34)
Don't Know	34.5(41)	45.5(10)	36.2(51)
No Opinion	6.7(8)	4.5(1)	6.4(9)
Total	82.6(119)	15.3(22)	97.9(141)[a]

[a]Remaining 2.1 percent work in northern Virginia.

Source: Metropolitan Washington Council of Governments, Transportation Planning Board, *Home Interview Survey* (Washington, 1968).

Table 2-11
How Can Transportation Best Be Improved, for One's Self
and Generally (In Percent)

	Self		General	
Solutions	Work	Other	Downtown	Suburbs
Better Downtown Parking	17.1(40)	19.0(45)	12.1(29)	25.6(62)[a]
Park and Ride Lots	12.4(29)	12.7(30)	23.4(56)	2.9(7)
Better Local Streets and Roads	7.3(17)	6.4(15)	7.1(17)	5.3(13)
More Freeways	7.3(17)	3.0(7)	4.2(10)	7.9(19)
Better Bus System	9.0(21)	11.0(26)	3.8(9)	15.7(38)
METRO	29.9(70)	16.9(40)	19.2(46)	21.1(51)
Provide Commuter Rail Service	16.2(38)	26.2(62)	27.6(66)	17.4(42)
Improve Taxi Service	0.9(2)	5.1(12)	2.5(6)	4.1(10)
Total	(234)	(237)	(239)	(242)

[a]Choice here is to provide more suburban parking facilities.

Source: Metropolitan Washington Council of Governments, Transportation Planning Board, *Home Interview Survey* (Washington, 1968).

At this point it appears that METRO is the preferred alternative only for the work trip, and even in that category it is not an overwhelming choice. Several points must be made in reference to the specific kind of service that METRO is trying to provide.

In the first place, some of the solutions mentioned are directly related to the provision of rapid transit kinds of service. A park and ride lot is nothing more than a large parking lot at a rapid transit stop so that people can drive from home to a transit station and then take a rapid transit vehicle downtown. Whether the transit vehicle is a bus or some kind of rail vehicle, the essence of park and ride is that it permits people to use rapid transit for the most congested part of their work trip.

As for the large showing of commuter rail service for all types of travel, it is important to note that the differences between rail rapid transit (METRO) and commuter rail service may not be entirely clear to people who have had little or no experience with either form of travel. With less than one-half of a percent of survey area respondents using a commuter rail system to get to work, it is entirely possible that at least part of the favorable attitude towards commuter rail service is attributable to METRO.

The relatively poor showing of METRO for non-work trips again points out that the system has been designed for the downtown oriented work trip and is at its best under such conditions.

As Figures 2-1 and 2-2 indicate, a rail transit system, such as the one being built in the Washington, D.C. area, that provides good coverage to downtown, provides poor service for trips headed to a suburban center. To explain further, a traveler headed downtown would be able to drive (or take a bus) from his home to a train station with little difficulty since all transit lines converge on downtown. Thus a person living at location number 1 would be able to choose from either of two transit lines for his trip to downtown depending on the distance of the stations from his home. Location 2 is equally well served by the rail system despite its being further from the downtown terminus. Finally, a person living at location 3 has a choice of two transit lines for his trip to downtown.

For the suburban trip, one can logically expect rail transit to be used for such trips only along a very narrow area along the rail line, with all other trips being made by bus or automobile. A person at location 1 would be able to travel to the transit line serving the suburban center and catch a train with little serious difficulty. Residents at locations 2 and 3 are much less able to do this. For them to travel to the suburban center would first require a trip to downtown and then a second trip via a train going to the suburban center.

In other words, because of the design of the METRO system, in the overwhelming majority of cases, travel downtown is more convenient and easier than travel to any suburban center.

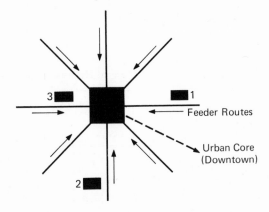

Figure 2-1. Travel to Downtown Via a Rail Rapid Transit System. Source: Richard H. Pratt, *Considerations in Rail Rapid Transit Route Planning*, presented to the WMATA Board of Directors (Washington, D.C.: Office of Planning and Finance, WMATA, 1967), p. 6.

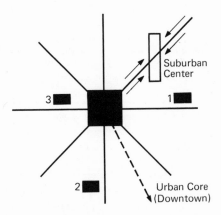

Figure 2-2. Travel to a Suburban Center Via a Rail Rapid Transit System: Source: See Figure 2-1.

Another possible explanation of the failure of METRO to capture the imagination of more area residents is prompted by a Louis Harris nationwide survey taken in March, 1968, concerning problems facing the cities.

Table 2-12

Relative Ranking of Urban Problems by Place of Residence, in Percent

Problem	Suburbs		Central City	
	Percent	Rank	Percent	Rank
Slums	51	3	49	2
Racial Tension	53	2	47	3
Crime on the Streets	72	1	73	1
Lack of Good Middle-Income Housing	17	6	16	6
Need for Better City Officials	25	5	20	5
Riots	30	4	36	4
Lack of Good Public Transportation	11	8	6	7
Too Much Overcrowding	14	7	8	8
Too Much Noise	2	9	1	9

Question: "Now I want to give you this card with some problems people feel are now facing the cities. If you had to choose, which two or three of these problems do you feel are the most important to solve in the cities of America." (March, 1968).

Source: U.S. Department of Housing and Urban Development, *A Profile of Suburbs and Central Cities in the United States*, fifth draft (unpublished report, August 1968).

As is quite evident, transportation problems do not rank high on a list of possible urban problems. In the city, transportation difficulties rank seventh out of a possible nine problems. The lack of importance attributed to transportation in general is seen in that the next highest mentioned problem, the need for good middle income housing, received more than twice as many mentions as did the need for better public transportation. For suburban residents, transportation ranks even lower on the spectrum of urban problems.

In response to the same kind of questions for our inner city neighborhoods, crime is the most often cited problem while transportation is considered to be of much lesser consequence. Table 2-13 provides the relevant data. For respondents

Table 2-13

Importance of Metropolitan Problems by Area in Percent

	N. Anacostia				S. Anacostia				Central City				Catholic Univ.-Ft. Lincoln				All Areas			
	First Choice		Second Choice		First Choice		Second Choice		First Choice		Second Choice		First Choice		Second Choice		First Choice		Second Choice	
	%	Rank	%	Rank	%	Rank	%	Rank	%	Rank	%	Rank	%	Rank	%	Rank	%	Rank	%	Rank
Air & Water Pollution	2.4	4	—	—	2.0	8	2.4	7	3.9	6	1.4	8	10.0	3	10.0	6	3.3	6	2.4	7
Unemployment	11.9	2	6.1	4	10.9	2	—	—	9.1	4	—	—	5.0	4	—	—	10.0	2	1.0	9
Education	11.9	2	3.0	5	5.0	5	9.6	6	10.4	2	8.7	4	15.0	2	20.0	1	8.7	3	9.3	5
Recreation	—	—	3.0	5	—	—	15.7	3	—	—	5.8	6	—	—	—	—	—	—	8.8	6
Crime	66.7	1	3.0	5	58.4	1	1.2	8	55.8	1	2.9	7	60.0	1	—	—	59.2	1	2.0	8
Housing	2.4	4	12.1	3	9.9	3	15.7	3	9.1	4	8.7	4	5.0	4	20.0	1	7.9	4	13.2	4
Poverty	2.4	4	24.2	2	4.0	6	20.5	1	1.3	7	17.4	3	—	—	15.0	4	2.5	7	19.5	3
Transportation	—	—	27.3	1	4.0	6	14.5	5	—	—	27.5	1	—	—	15.0	4	1.7	8	21.0	2
Can't Say	2.4	4	—	—	5.9	4	20.5	1	10.4	2	27.5	1	—	—	20.0	1	6.7	5	22.9	1

Source: Metropolitan Washington Council of Government, Transportation Planning Board, *Home Interview Survey*, (Washington, 1968).

in each of the four neighborhoods, crime is by far the most often cited problem in the metropolitan area. Moreover, the range of opinion on this issue is quite close in all four areas, indicating a general consensus on the seriousness of the crime problem. After crime, agreement on area wide problems rapidly decreases to a point at which the second most mentioned problem, unemployment, receives only 10 percent of all possible mentions. There is agreement on transportation problems as it ranks last on the list of problems facing the metropolitan area, receiving less than 2 percent of all responses.

When residents are asked to name the second most important problem facing the metropolitan area, the response pattern changes completely. Crime drops from first to last while transportation receives the greatest response rate of any specific problem selected. What is surprising is that 22.9 percent of all respondents cannot mention a second specific problem facing the Washington, D.C. metropolitan area.

Conclusion

This chapter has attempted to analyze the present transportation system in the Washington, D.C. metropolitan area, and provide some insight as to the potential success of METRO. In addition, a substantial effort has been made to discover the transportation preferences of inner city residents and rank those preferences according to a list of possible areawide problems. One of the major findings was that the majority of inner city respondents find their work trip convenient, but that a large minority are critical of their work trip. By mode of travel it was quite clear that people who relied on the bus were much more critical of their travel than were automobile users. Part of the reason for the discontent with the bus is attributable to the long travel times required for most trips by area respondents. Although the data presented are for suburban trips, data are available for all trips regardless of destination.

Better than half (57 percent) of all Washington, D.C. residents who drive to work get to their place of employment in twenty-five minutes or less. On the other hand, 78 percent of those using the bus spend twenty-six minutes or longer getting to work, and 52 percent of those using two or more buses require more than forty-five minutes to get to work.[36]

In trying to determine the potential use of METRO the data revealed that potential use was closely tied to the degree of satisfaction with the present mode of travel to work, but that a significant group do not know whether or not they will use the new system, regardless of the quality of their present journey to work.

As for the transportation preferences of the respondents, METRO is the most mentioned for the work trip, the purpose for which it was designed. Once non-work trips are introduced into the picture, the preference for METRO declines as its ability to serve non-downtown, non-rush hour travel decreases.

The survey data show that for most inner city respondents, transportation is not a top priority concern, but that it is important especially to users of public transportation.

But the large percentage of "don't knows" when survey area respondents were asked if they thought they would patronize METRO for the work trip indicates that improvements in existing transportation facilities or wider automobile ownership might meet inner city travel needs better than METRO appears to meet them. At any rate, METRO is not a grass roots demand among the respondents of the inner city Washington, D.C. neighborhoods used in this research.

The actual importance that inner city residents attach to transportation or the anxiety with which they view their own immobility are less important from a long range perspective than is how well METRO will fit in with and is related to development in the National Capital area. Metropolitan growth and development is generally taking place outside the central city. The central city as a place of employment is declining when compared to outside central city areas. Washington, D.C. has traditionally been a professional and service oriented city, and current trends indicate that this pattern will continue.

In view of the region's unique employment base and the development trends operating here and throughout the rest of the nation, the only place for blue-collar and semiskilled jobs to locate and grow is in the suburbs.

METRO, however, is not designed to encourage or serve such growth since it has been specifically designed to serve downtown Washington, D.C. What this means is that the area with the greatest growth potential will receive less comprehensive service than will downtown, but this is almost a requirement of METRO in view of the technology and design adopted by system officials.

3

Evolution of the METRO System: Phase 1

The official birth of the METRO system, the National Capital region's answer to rail rapid transit, came on December 9, 1969, when President Richard M. Nixon signed legislation authorizing Federal participation in a ninety-eight mile regional transit system to the extent of $1.147 billion over a ten year period. This simple act was preceded by almost a quarter of a century of planning and political decisions which often changed the scope and extent of the system.

As in any major public policy undertaking, the process by which the National Capital area got a subway involved numerous actors, many heterogeneous and sometimes incompatible interests, and greater or lesser degrees of commitment and involvement by the participants. In addition, certain groups and interests were intimately involved throughout the entire process, while other interests and actors came into the process at a later date and contended for the rewards of METRO service for a shorter period.

One result was that some participants were able to influence basic service, financial, and planning decisions, decisions which became constraints upon the subsequent influence of later participants.

Meyerson and Banfield in studying public housing decisions in Chicago likened the process to a " ... game in which each player adds a word to a sentence which is passed around the circle of players...."[1] However, the Chicago housing authority staff played part of the game bound by the previous moves of Congress, the U.S. Public Housing Administration, Illinois legislature and state housing authority, and finally the Mayor and City Council.[2] The responsibility of the staff of the housing authority was to "... finish the sentence in a way that would seem to be rational...."[3]

The players in the METRO game represented the same kinds of interests as the Chicago group. In the Nation's Capital, Congress, the suburbs, freeway forces, the bus company owners, planners given the responsibility of designing the system, and the general public, all added to the effort that eventually was to become METRO. But the final form of METRO was very much the result of some early decisions that set what were accepted as unchangeable conditions.

"Washington: Present and Future" Through the Mass Transportation Survey: 1950-1959

In April, 1950, the National Capital Planning Commission (NCPC) issued "A General Summary of the Comprehensive Plan for the Nation's Capital and Its

47

Environs," titled *Washington: Present and Future*. A month later the transportation portion of the plan was issued as a brochure *Moving People and Goods*. The transportation findings were summarized as follows:

The major problem in connection with local traffic circulation in Washington is found within and adjacent to the central area. This is caused by the super-imposition of heavy federal employment upon the central business district, creating a concentration greater than that of the usual city. In this area streets are now used to about 80 percent of capacity; traffic movement is slow and difficult, particularly because of the funneling of many streetcars through a few intersections. *While the total volume of transit cannot be expected to increase, other vehicular movement is estimated to increase about 30 percent by 1980.*[4] (emphasis supplied)

The attention paid to mobility problems in the 1950 plan also found expression in the National Capital Planning Act of 1952 which directed the NCPC and the National Capital Regional Planning Council (NCRPC) to prepare comprehensive plans for land use, major thoroughfares, and the movement of people and goods in the region.

The transportation portion of the mandate was realized in the Second Supplemental Appropriations Act of 1955[5] which provided funds for the NCPC and the NCRPC to "jointly conduct a survey of the present and future mass transportation needs of the National Capital region . . . and to report their findings and recommendations to the President, . . ."[6]

As the survey progressed, a Joint Steering Committee appointed by the NCPC and NCRPC to conduct the survey authorized the release of a series of supporting documents compiled by consultants under contract to the Committee. In June, 1955, the Committee recommended that the initial work of the survey should be the preparation of a general development plan for the region as a basis for the mass transportation plan.[7]

Soon after, a $19,000 contract was entered into with the Council for Economic and Industry Research (CEIR) for a limited economic base study, comprehensive enough in scope to be used to project population growth, employment and land use within the region for 1965 and 1980.

While the consultant studies continued, the Congress in 1957 created a Joint Committee on Washington Metropolitan Problems (JCWMP), under the chairmanship of Senator Alan Bible. This Committee conducted a comprehensive survey of metropolitan problems apart from the transportation activities of the NCPC and NCRPC, investigating such areas as water supply, sewage disposal, land use, economic development, intergovernmental relations, and transportation problems. The Committee launched an intensive inquiry into the status and prospects of the mass transportation survey with the initial result of this inquiry being an April, 1958, staff report "Metropolitan Transportation" by Arthur Lazarus.[8]

The report was an analysis of all that had gone on in the survey, and pointed out both the accomplishments and inadequacies of the reports thus far published.

Lazarus found that the whole orientation of the survey was determined by its location in the two general planning agencies, and that this perspective did not allow for much participation by existing transportation interests, by the business community, banking and investment interests, or by many other people who would necessarily be involved if any specific action steps were going to be taken. Thus he suggested that further efforts were needed to:

(1) investigate the motivations of potential mass transit users in an auto-dominant community;
(2) explore the technology of new modes of transportation;
(3) investigate the interaction between land use and transit design;
(4) secure the cooperation of Congress, Maryland and Virginia officials, and District representatives; and
(5) secure the cooperation of transit operators, parking agencies, planning agencies, and business and financial interests.[9]

In January, 1959, three more reports, which ultimately were to form the core of the entire transportation program, were issued by the Steering Committee. The first report, by Wilbur Smith and Associates of New Haven, Connecticut, was a traffic engineering study[10] which undertook to forecast metropolitan travel volumes in 1965 and 1980, trip time, and mode selection.

The second report, a civil engineering study by DeLeuw, Cather & Co. of Chicago, was the product of the single most important contract let by the mass transportation survey.[11] The contract defined the duties of the engineers as: providing support for the preliminary plans provided by the mass transportation survey staff; offering suggestions for supplementing, combining, amending, or eliminating aspects of the survey staff's plans; developing an estimated bill for construction and financing; but not developing a fully articulated plan or system.[12]

The DeLeuw, Cather report presented costs and revenues for several alternative transportation systems in accordance with certain hypotheses developed by the Joint Steering Committee of the mass transportation survey. The first alternative, an auto-dominant system, consisted of an extensive network of freeways, parkways, and arterial streets along with large-scale downtown parking facilities on the assumption that a steadily increasing proportion of people would use private automobiles. Public transportation would consist of buses sharing streets with other automotive traffic as in the present system. An express bus system, consisting of high-speed buses making few stops and traveling on freeways, parkways, and their own rights-of-way, was the second alternative. Local buses would supplement the express service, and highways or parking facilities would be somewhat less than in the auto-based plan. The third alternative was a rail transit dominant plan with local buses, highways, and parking facilities assuming much the same character as they did under the express bus plan. A fourth plan, providing for the optimum integration of all modes of transportation, was developed by DeLeuw, Cather and eventually became the "recommended system."

The third support study was the *Preliminary Financial and Organizational Report* of the Institute for Public Administration (IPA). It is interesting to note that this was the only one of the support studies not published by the Joint Steering Committee. Although the Committee cited the lack of funds as the reason, investigation of the proceedings of the Joint Steering Committee indicates that they disagreed with certain organizational alternatives put forth by the IPA, and did not want to publish the report.

The Institute proposed the creation of a transportation organization closely related to an effective regional planning agency, embracing all forms of transportation, and having arrangements for responsiveness to the governing officials of the region.[13]

Finally, in July of 1959, the long-awaited *Transportation Plan for the National Capital Region* made its public appearance.[14] The plan made four recommendations to meet the Washington area's transportation needs between 1960 and 1980:

(1) construction of a network of freeways on which people could travel quickly between any two points in the region even at hours when traffic was heaviest;
(2) high-speed bus service leading to downtown along freeways and parkways, and the creation of a rail transit system to serve downtown and extending outward to Silver Spring, Bethesda, Alexandria, and Anacostia;
(3) improved arterial streets and highways to carry automotive traffic not carried by the freeways; and,
(4) expanded and improved local transit service on arterial and local streets to carry passengers not served by new bus and rail facilities.[15]

The recommended system consisted of 33 miles of rail rapid transit, 66 miles of express bus routes, and parking facilities for the rail and bus routes all totaling $564 million.

The freeway portion of the plan, costing $1.8 billion, called for 329 miles of new freeways and expressways and $119 million worth of downtown parking facilities, in addition to the 81 miles of freeways already in existence.[16] Total cost of the system was thus estimated at $2.5 billion.[17]

Transportation Plan for the National Capital Region to the "Whitener Plan": 1959-1963

Media

Immediate reaction to the publication of the Mass Transportation Survey (MTS) came from the Washington, D.C. newspapers. In a July 12, 1959 editorial the *Sunday Star* said:

... the Report makes a great number of assumptions about the willingness and capability of both the Federal and local governments to perform certain functions. These assumptions involve policy decisions that will not be reached easily or quickly.... The transportation report ... should be regarded as a starting point rather than as a final product. Accepted this way, it can be an invaluable document.[18]

The *Washington Post* in its editorial on the same day basically agreed with the *Star* and added that as a starting point the report was "intelligent, balanced, and thoroughgoing."[19] As to the actual scope and nature of the plan, the *Post* had some reservations proceeding directly from the part of the plan which recommended that the transportation system should consist of freeways "on which people can travel quickly between any two parts of the region, even at hours when traffic is heaviest."[20] The editorial concluded that:

in all humility before the imponderables and uncontrollables of the business of urban life and growth, we feel compelled to ask, what kind of city planning is this?
The idea that the urban resident and taxpayer really desires or is willing to pay for the total fluidity of movement which the report seems to envisage strikes us as a rather shallow judgement.
Is it the business of the general public to provide such facilities for the minority who deliberately choose to live at great distances from their place of employment? ... it does not follow that the most whimsical desires of every citizen on this matter should be justified by a very costly transportation system.[21]

The Washington Post in an October editorial objected to the desires of some highway enthusiasts who wanted to "turn Washington into concrete."[22]
The editorial pointed out:

if some road enthusiasts had their way, the District would soon resemble nothing so much as an enormous airport apron. Parks, residences, nothing is sacred in the march of "progress" that has as its ostensibly highest aim the building of universal monuments to the automobile civilization. To what purpose this bringing of more and more cars into the city to hurry up and wait? ... Unless

Washington planners and officials and community leaders come together on a project that is both desirable and possible and then join in energetic endeavor to achieve it, the happy highwayman will take over by default.[23]

Congress

The Joint Committee under Senator Bible began a lengthy series of hearings on the mass transportation survey plan. From the hearings it seemed apparent, (1) that the appeal of a rail transit system had been underestimated in the study and, (2) that there was great local opposition to the effect that new highways would have on the community.

The list of witnesses testifying in favor of the rail portion of the plan was impressive, and had a significant impact on subsequent congressional actions. The following statements are typical of the testimony given at the hearings:

"We should like to stress the importance of giving the highest priority to development of the proposed rail transit facilities to reduce travel time and avoid unnecessary costs."—Elmer B. Statts, Deputy Director, Bureau of the Budget, for the Administration.[24] "I think highways have great use, but I believe that the program we are talking about here overemphasizes these superhighways into the heart of Washington."—Roy W. Johnson, Chairman, American Council to Improve Our Neighborhoods (ACTION).

"The survey is basically statistical, and if its recommendations are fully carried out, it will result in a mechanical situation without beauty, peace, or pollution-free air."—Grosvenor Chapman, Washington Metropolitan Chapter, American Institute of Architects.[25]

As a result of these hearings, the Bureau of the Budget, acting for the President, and consulting with state and local government, prepared legislation to establish the transportation agency called for in the 1959 plan. This legislation was enacted as the National Capital Transportation Act of 1960.[26] The National Capital Transportation Agency (NCTA) created by the act was directed by Congress to evaluate the 1959 plan, to consider alternatives to the plan that might be less costly and damaging to the city, to coordinate transportation planning in the region, and to report their findings to the President no later than November 1, 1962. Congress had stated as a matter of policy that there should be planning on a regional basis of a unified system of freeways and parkways, express transit on exclusive rights-of-way, and other major transportation facilities.

Congress also directed the NCTA to prepare a Transit Development Program as a prelude to the construction of transportation facilities,[27] and empowered the Agency, subject to congressional approval, to construct and provide for the operation of mass transit facilities.[28]

The Transit Development Program was to consist of a plan indicating the general location of transit facilities to be developed by the NCTA; a timetable for the construction of those facilities; and comprehensive financial statements showing costs, revenues, and benefits of the proposed system.[29] In developing a program, Congress required the Agency to give special attention to expanding the use of existing facilities and services, and to early development of a subway from Union Station to the principal employment centers in the District, a subway capable of being extended to serve other parts of the region.[30]

Congress decided that the costs of the system should be borne as much as possible by those using or benefitting from the transportation facilities. The House District of Columbia Committee Report specifically stated that the subway system must be designed so that it did not require or need continued Federal financing.[31]

The record also shows that Congress did not look at the transportation plan as a finished document but rather as a starting point. For this reason they provided for more detailed studies in the Transit Development Plan.[32] At the same time, by giving the NCTA the power to acquire or construct transit facilities,[33] Congress indicated that the need for more studies was no substitute for action, especially where action was necessary for the accomplishment of long range goals.[34]

Work went on in earnest at the NCTA for the next eighteen months. From April 1961 to November 1962, the study staff with the assistance of several outside consultants completed the review of the 1959 plan and prepared its own report.

But during this time the NCTA conferred little with other planning, citizen, or business groups, so that when in November 1962 the NCTA report[35] and recommendations were made public, it was the first time many local groups had seen them.

In terms of importance for the shape of a transit system, the major finding of the NCTA report was that the region's transportation crisis was in part due to its rapidly growing population, and in part due to governmental policies which encouraged suburban growth.

The NCTA also found that the downtown area would continue to remain the largest single employment area in the region with an increasing number of work trips to and through downtown.[36] These findings prompted a call for increasing the thirty-three miles of rail transit in the 1959 plan to eighty-three miles, and cutting the size of the freeway program from 410 to 255 miles.[a] The "heart" of the rail system was to be a nineteen mile subway network so routed that eight of every ten downtown workers would be within a five minute walk of a subway station.[37]

---

[a]The 1962 plan called for fifty miles of new freeways in addition to the 205 miles in use or under construction.

The pattern of the downtown system was guided by existing and potential development of the downtown area and was designed to provide "convenient circulation between all major concentrations of downtown activity,"[38] including Federal, commercial, and office sites.

However, aware of the congressional mandate that the system pay for itself and not require continuous Federal Government funding,[39] the report, emphatically stated that:

the proposed regional rapid transit system can pay all operating expenses. . . . It can do so because the region has a heavily occupied downtown area and . . . because projected use of railroad rights-of-way and freeway medians will reduce the capital outlay required.[40]

In the early days of developing a transit plan that would best meet the needs of the region, the NCTA was primarily concerned with how to provide good service throughout downtown. A principal reason for this was that Congress had directed the NCTA to consider a downtown subway, but also because in the foreseeable future downtown Washington, D.C. would continue to be the largest single employment center in the entire region.

The primary goal of the downtown lines was to place stations (service) as close to as many jobs as possible; qualified by the need to keep expensive in-town subway construction to a minimum, and by the desire for high-speed service. The secondary goal of the downtown lines was to service the off-peak traveler.[41]

In justifying its plan the NCTA claimed the following advantages over the 1959 MTS study:

(1) the MTS plan would not provide satisfactory service to such growth areas as Prince Georges, Arlington, and Fairfax Counties. The NCTA felt that projected traffic volumes justified rail service to these areas while the 1959 plan provided them with express bus service;

(2) capital outlays for the system would be $367 million less under the NCTA plan;

(3) annual operating costs for the highways under the NCTA plan would be $2.5 million as opposed to $5.1 million under MTS;

(4) fewer people, 540, would be displaced in the District of Columbia under the NCTA proposal than under the MTS plan (33,000); and

(5) taxable land taken by the transit system would be almost 75 percent less under the NCTA plan; $0.5 million to $1.9 million.[42]

The proposed rail transit system would cost $793 million. Of the eighty-three miles of rail transit, seven lines would consist of rapid transit and one would be commuter railroad service, all servicing major travel corridors in the region.

Figures 3-1 and 3-2 show the similarities and differences between the 1959 MTS plan and the 1962 eighty-three mile proposal of the NCTA.

The NCTA pointed out that the eight transit lines:

will extend into the most heavily populated sections of the District and the suburbs, ... [and] have been planned to service the greatest number of people—and thereby generate as much revenue as possible per dollar of capital outlay— ...[43]

On May 27, 1963, the NCTA program, with strong presidential endorsement, was sent to Congress, along with recommended legislation authorizing construction of the facilities called for in the NCTA plan. In July, fifty-four witnesses, including representatives of the federal, state, and local governments in the region, planning agencies, business and civic groups, private transit companies, and a number of private citizens, testified at seven days of hearings on the plan. In addition, a number of outside consultant studies were available to the committee covering engineering, route locations, right-of-way acquisition, analysis of alternate transportation systems, studies of commuter attitudes toward rapid transit, traffic forecasts, and operating costs and revenue estimates.

The hearings pointed out several interesting and potentially volatile differences over the NCTA plan.

On one hand it was patently clear that federal, state, and local officials, most planning groups, and the public at large supported the plan. As pointed out by the House District of Columbia Committee: "the public regards the need for a system of rapid rail transit as a matter of the greatest urgency both to meet the volumes of traffic and to maintain the beauty of the Capital."[44]

At the other extreme were the highway proponents. In its report the NCTA had recommended the construction of certain freeways and highways, although nowhere in its legislation was the Agency given specific authority to undertake highway planning. This recommendation curtailed and revised highway plans advocated by road user groups. At the hearings, the NCTA highway recommendations were subjected to strong attack and they became one of the focal points of opposition to the transit system. In addition, President Kennedy in his message to Congress supporting the NCTA plan called for a re-evaluation of certain controversial highway projects and asked for special study of the highway projects.[45]

The resulting re-evaluation stopped most of the interstate highway projects in the District of Columbia and helped to polarize the participants into highway supporters and subway supporters.

At this point highway user groups got involved. Their position was summarized in the following quote from *The Highway User*:

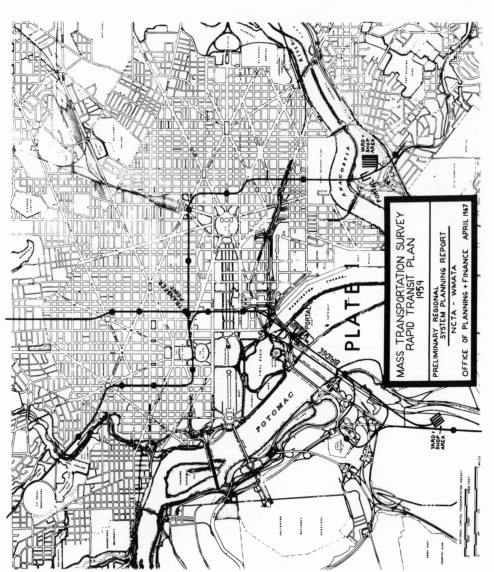

Figure 3–1. Rapid Transit Plan, 1959.

57

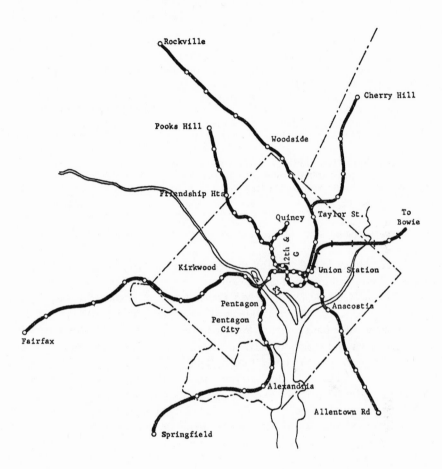

Figure 3–2. Eighty-Three Mile Regional Transit System. Source: U.S. Congress, House, Committee on the District of Columbia, *Transit Program for the National Capital Region*, Supplement to Hearings before Subcommittee No. 6 of the Committee on the District of Columbia on H.R. 6633, H.R. 7249, and H.R. 8929, 88th Cong., 1st Sess., p. 3.

In addition to the importance of the suspended highway projects in the Nation's Capital from the standpoint of representing a broken link in the Interstate System, the Washington controversy has far-reaching implications for still another reason.

In at least one of the publications issued by the National Capital Transporation Agency appeared this paragraph:

"The Nation's Capital, because of its unique relationship to the country, can well be considered a model area. The mass transportation system of this area will have the same character. It is imperative that what is done . . . must be done well. The 212 metropolitan areas of this country will look upon the National Capital Transportation Agency and its work as a model from which they can draw knowledge to help them in their growing problems of mass transportation."

Highway users feel that the inference to be drawn from this is obvious: that the campaign to supplant freeways with subways in Washington is the opening gun in what could lead to a national movement to slow down or curtail the highway program.[46]

Other significant opposition came from the bus companies operating in the region.

Representatives of D.C. Transit, the region's largest bus company, Alexandria, Barcroft and Washington Transit Company (A. B. & W.), and Washington, Virginia, and Maryland (W. V. & M.) Transit Company argued that bus service could equal or surpass the recommended rail system, would be more flexible, and would provide better service. Similar to their testimony at earlier hearings, they supported additional freeways and highways with reserved bus lanes and opposed any concept of a "feeder bus" system.

D.C. Transit pointed to the legislation passed by Congress in 1956[47] giving that company exclusive right to operate all public transportation in Washington, D.C. The company concluded that unless Congress repealed D.C. Transit's franchise, it had similar privileges relative to the proposed rail system. Finally, the American Automobile Association and the Bureau of Public Roads testified against the plan. It thus became evident at the hearings that the significant opposition to the rail plan came from highway users and their supporting groups.

Between July and November, 1963, a great deal of mystery surrounded the transit program, as it was not until December that the House Committee filed its report on the plan—in the form of a completely new bill.[48] From the hearings it appears that members of the Committee had reservations about the practicality and viability of the eighty-three mile system; especially as it related to the system's ability to generate enough patronage to be self-supporting. At any rate, in a supplement to the July hearings a new bill, H.R. 8929, introduced by Representative Basil Whitener (D-N.C.) was made public.

The Whitener bill authorized the NCTA to construct a 23.3 mile subway rail rapid transit system, largely within the confines of the District of Columbia, but extending to such suburban areas as Woodside (Montgomery County), the Pentagon, and Rosslyn (Arlington County). The bill also authorized the creation of a commuter rail line from Union Station at the Capital to Bowie, Maryland, along Pennsylvania Railroad rights-of-way. Despite a decrease in rail coverage of almost 72 percent (83 to 23.3 miles), the estimated cost of the smaller system decreased by only 49 percent ($793 million to $400.6 million). This was largely due to the elimination of the lower cost suburban routes. Figure 3-3 depicts the 23.3 mile system introduced by Rep. Whitener.

In justifying its proposal, the Committee noted that in addition to a large amount of public support for the NCTA system, there were also serious uncertainties in the minds of some suburban jurisdictions as to the precise location of rail lines outside the District of Columbia. Therefore, following discussions with NCTA representatives, the Committee decided that the most appropriate procedure at that point would be to secure approval of an abbreviated portion of the system, mainly within the District of Columbia.[49]

The Committee also stated that the eighty-three mile program was based on estimates for the region in the year 1980, estimates that could be significantly affected by changing land use or developmental patterns. Thus it was unnecessary to commit the Federal Government to the full regional system at this time.[50]

The National Capital region was still not destined to get rail rapid transit, for on December 9, 1963, the House of Representatives voted 278 to 87 to recommit the bill to committee.[51] The floor debate reveals that battle lines were drawn over benefits to be realized from the system versus certain inadequacies in the legislation. System proponents talked about preservation of the aesthetic values of the city from further despoilation by the automobile, and about regional growth, while opponents concentrated on the lack of protection given to labor, the plan's apparent advocacy of public ownership and operation of the system, and the apparent lack of a ceiling on Federal Government spending for the system.

As for the labor provision, opponents argued that no provision had been made for collective bargaining, job security, or any of several other labor rights. To this, supporters replied that no such provisions were included because they were premature. Supporters held that the most pressing need was for construction and that there was no need to delay this phase of the program since several years were available to take care of the other considerations.

Representative Multer (D-N.Y.) opposed the twenty-three mile system on private enterprise grounds. It was his feeling that in failing specifically to provide for private operation of the subway system, government operation was conceded. This he felt was another step on the road to "big" government and was anti-private enterprise. He further argued that because the people planning

SYSTEM AUTHORIZED BY SUBSTITUTE BILL (H.R. 8929)

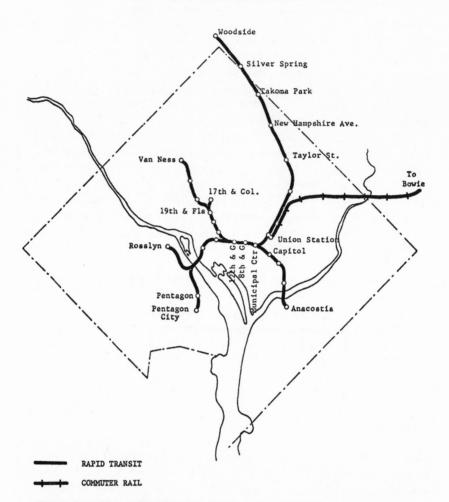

RAPID TRANSIT

COMMUTER RAIL

Figure 3-3. 23.3 Mile Whitener Plan. Source: U.S. Congress, House, Committee on the District of Columbia, *Transit Program for the National Capital Region*, Supplement to Hearings before Subcommittee No. 6 of the District of Columbia on H.R. 6633, H.R. 7249, and H.R. 8929, 88th Cong., 1st Sess., p. 4.

the system did not think of private enterprise they were "utterly incompetent" as planners.[52] Representative O'Konski (R-Wisc.) opposed the system on the grounds that the expense was out of proportion to the benefits of the venture. He compared the estimated $400.6 million construction cost for the system to a $325 million rapid transit grant program for the nation, and concluded that since the House defeated such an expenditure for the nation, it should do likewise for a "speck" like Washington.[53]

The *Washington Post* attempted to explain the defeat in a December 11 editorial:

Mr. Stolzenbach (NCTA Administrator) committed three errors of political judgement. He believed that he could build the subway only by vehemently attacking the (freeway). He believed that he could build the subway only if revenue estimates promised to pay the whole cost; the figures were demonstrably incredible. He believed that he could build the subway only by refusing to answer questions, however legitimate. He offered no assurance to the bus companies that he proposed to displace, or to their employees.

. . . The vote in the House was a sharp and explicit personal repudiation of Mr. Stolzenbach. . . . He can now serve the city best by resigning. He is so widely distrusted that it is doubtful if any bill can succeed while he retains office. A new administrator will have to work out, in detail, the relationship between the bus companies and the transit system, protecting the interests of the companies and their employees. He will have to meet and dispose of the absurd proposal for private ownership; one might as well talk of private ownership . . . of the sewers.[54]

The defeat of the Whitener proposal was taken without directions for change or amendment by the House. This, plus the size of the defeat, made it clear that the House would not pass a similar proposal unless there were some significant changes in the financing and operating parts of the plan.[55]

Evaluation

The evolution of METRO from 1958 to 1963 was directed and controlled almost entirely by Congress through the Joint Committee on Washington Metropolitan Problems.

Beginning with the 1958 *Metropolitan Transportation* Report and ending with the House defeat of a 23.3 mile rail rapid transit plan in 1963, Congress made, or influenced, the making of several crucial policy decisions.

The hostility and opposition with which the 1959 MTS plan was greeted by Congress, the media, and the public, culminated in the creation of the NCTA to re-do what was to have been done in the MTS study-survey the present and future mass transportation needs of the National Capital region. The refusal of both people and government to accept the MTS findings was based on a relatively simple fact; for five years they had believed that a mass transportation survey was being taken that would lead to a regional transit network serving the entire area. What came out instead was the highway plan described earlier.

Although the public demand for a rail rapid transit system was clearly established in the 1959 hearings, less clear was the kind of system preferred by Congress, the ultimate source of most planning and construction funds.

While Congress gave the NCTA a free hand in planning much of the transit system, it did create several unalterable conditions that affected all future work. Most important was the requirement that any transit system be financially self-sufficient.

What this came to mean was that all route planning had to be primarily concerned with revenue production and less with social welfare or urban redevelopment effects. This is not to say that service and revenue production are incompatible ends, or that all social goals were ignored in designing as profitable a system as possible. One of the best ways to make any transportation system financially sound is to make it more attractive to the consumer than competitive modes. (The decline of public transportation during the last thirty years can be greatly attributed to the mode choices available to the consumer. In no city in the United States has the commuter been able to choose between a shiny new automobile and a shiny new mass transit system. To date, choices have been between private, comfortable, demand oriented automobiles, and smelly, noisy, unpredictable mass transit.) However, the congressionally imposed fare-box priority did not allow for much consideration of the travel requirements of the non-automobile owning segment of society.

The demise of the NCTA's eighty-three mile regional system can be viewed as too much rail transit at the wrong time. While the Agency interpreted the 1960 legislation as a mandate to plan a regional transit network, Congress was not ready to go that far in bringing a rail rapid transit system to the National Capital area.

Congressional intent was quite clear from the 1960 act. In addition to the financial constraints posed, rail transit was to focus on the downtown portion of Washington, D.C. and be capable of being expanded into a regional system. The NCTA eighty-three mile system failed to meet these requirements.

The substitute plan created in committee by Rep. Whitener was downtown oriented, was expandable, and was financially self-supporting (according to official pronouncements). However, the substitute measure failed to gain the enthusiastic support of the public and other interests that had pushed for the regional system. In addition, the entire House of Representatives had its first opportunity to vote on something concrete in relation to the subway issue. Previous legislative action had been on appropriations for the MTS and NCTA study budgets. The lack of enthusiastic support and the opposition presented by freeway and bus interests, and by congressional critics resulted in the defeat of the 23.3 mile substitute measure.

Opposition to rail rapid transit by the freeway groups (especially the American Automobile Association) was not based so much on opposition to mass transit, but upon resentment against being cut out of the transportation picture. The 1959 MTS plan was a freeway plan. Almost two billion dollars of the estimated $2.5 billion cost was for new freeways and parking facilities.

Rail transit was limited to thirty-three miles, mainly within the District of Columbia. Public and official opposition to the "concretizing" of much of the Nation's Capital brought quick response from the American Automobile Association in a supplementary statement to their testimony:

It is clearly evident that commercial and selfish interests took advantage of the opportunity to appear before your committee to exploit their pet projects at the sacrifice of the public interest.

... Public opinion is confused and the controversies generated by certain commercial interests cloud the real intent of the basic transportation survey....

Let it be kept constantly in mind that the program for the future of metropolitan Washington's traffic pattern is based solidly on expressway construction as the No. 1 goal. Express buses and rapid rail transit are foreseen as potential future possibilities. But the major message of the report is the essentiality of building highway and street facilities for automotive transport at the earliest possible moment.[56]

The NCTA's regional proposal, completely reordering these priorities alienated the highway forces. In addition, President Kennedy in halting most of the freeway projects in the District of Columbia pending further study added more fuel to the smoldering fire.

Thus when the regional plan was scrapped and the substitute measure failed to arouse much support, the freeway groups were able to make their displeasure at the new priorities felt on Capitol Hill.

As for the bus companies, O. Roy Chalk, President and owner of D.C. Transit, the region's largest public carrier said that: ". . . we are in favor of a modern rapid transit system. . ." but, "we are in favor of private enterprise being continued indefinitely as the exclusive operator of any transit system in the Nation's Capital. . .", and "we are violently opposed to the extravagance of public ownership and operation, and the illegal violation of S. 3073 (the legislation granting Chalk his franchise)."[57] The intent of D.C. Transit becomes readily clear—any kind of public transit system in the Nation's Capital is acceptable as long as D.C. Transit owned and/or operated it.

4 Evolution of the METRO System: Phase 2

A Modified Rail System: 1965

Fourteen months after the defeat of the twenty-three mile system, the NCTA was ready to try again. This time they were given authority to "... design, engineer, construct, equip, and take other action ..."[1] to insure the creation of a rail rapid transit system described in the report *Rail Rapid Transit for the Nation's Capital.*[2]

The system described in this report was a 25 mile, $431 million rail system mainly within the District of Columbia, of which 13.1 miles was to be subway. The similarities between the 1963 and 1965 plans were great, but the differences between the two plans were sufficient to get the proposal through Congress.

Physically, the most noticeable change between the two plans was the re-routing of the Capitol-Anacostia route to serve the area around D.C. Stadium, the Armory, and D.C. General Hospital. In effect, this change served a more built-up area of the city assuring a better return per dollar of capital investment, but at the same time, it removed from direct rail service a large number of poor people.

Other changes in routing consisted of moving the Pentagon route up the Potomac River so that the Pentagon, Pentagon City, and Rosslyn could all be served by one line, instead of the line and branching operation in the 1963 plan. The Union Station-Bowie, Maryland commuter rail line was eliminated entirely from the 1965 plan on the grounds that patronage estimates did not justify its expense. Finally, the Columbia Heights line was extended from its 1963 terminus at 18th Street and Columbia Road N.W. to the intersection of Georgia and New Hampshire Avenues N.W. Figure 4-1 presents the 1965 modified rail transit plan.

The financial and organization changes in the 1965 plan seemed more important from the congressional view than the route changes. A re-reading of the 1963 debate clearly shows that the opposition to the plan was based on finance, organization, and labor grounds; not on service levels.

Of the $431 million capital cost of the system, the District of Columbia would be responsible for one-third of the revenue bond underwriting and one-third of the money raised by grants.[3] The 1963 financing plan called for 65 percent of all financing to be done by revenue bonds with the Federal

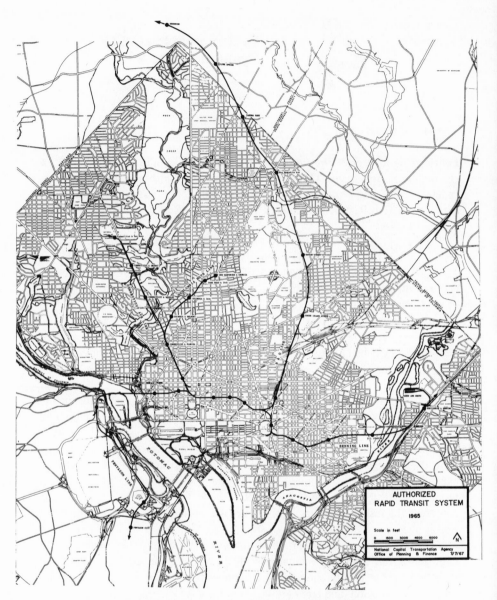

Figure 4–1. Twenty-Five Mile Basic Plan, 1965.

Government underwriting the principal and interest of the entire amount, some $258 million. The remaining $141.7 million would have come from a $120 million Federal grant and a $27.1 million District of Columbia grant. Obviously the result of all of this was that the Federal Government's share of the financing was significantly lessened while the District of Columbia was required to assume a larger share of the burden.[a]

Organizationally, the 1963 plan was silent on the matter of how the system should be operated; i.e. should NCTA operate the system as a public project, or should it be turned over to private enterprise and run as a profit making venture.

As noted earlier, sponsors of the 1963 legislation saw no problem in this and were willing to wait until construction had started before trying to solve this serious problem. Opponents attacked this stand as advocating a larger governmental role in traditionally private functions. Thus the 1965 plan specifically required that the rail system created under the legislation ". . . not be operated except under contract by private transit companies, private railroads, or other private persons."[4]

It was further specified that before any operating contracts could be signed, any and all interested and qualified persons "including private mass transportation companies in the National Capital region,"[b] had been permitted to indicate an interest and bid on the service.

Once the above changes had been made, the legislation easily passed both houses of Congress by voice vote during the Summer of 1965.

At this stage in the evolution of METRO, Congress had approved a twenty-five mile subway system within the District of Columbia but had not appropriated any funds for its actual construction. In fact, all that was given to the NCTA was $6.1 million in supplemental appropriations for more detailed planning, specific plans for bond issuance, station placement in Maryland and Virginia, and fare agreements with the local bus companies.

Evaluation

The modified rail rapid transit system passed by Congress is significant for policy making beyond the immediate problem of rail transit for the National Capital

[a]A comparison of the financing plans for the 1963 and 1965 rail transit systems shows the increased financial responsibility required of the District of Columbia in the 1965 plan: (in millions of dollars)

	1963 Federal Government	1965 District of Columbia	Federal Government	District of Columbia
Bonds	$258.9	---	$222.0	$111
Grants	$120.0	$21.7	$100.0	$50
Total	$378.9	$21.7	$322.0	$161

[b]This clause has been interpreted by some, this writer included, as protecting the interests of D.C. Transit, the largest bus company in the region.

region. As noted, congressional interest in service levels was of lesser importance than the financial and other considerations which led to the defeat of the 1963 plan. Thus, the changes made by the NCTA were just enough to get the plan through Congress and not enough to create new controversies by proposing a radically new system or by changing service priorities.

The nature of the 1965 plan also points out the incremental nature of the decision-making process of the project. The original plan was new, innovative, and regional in scope. Congressional intent, however, was to begin with a relatively small, downtown oriented system which could be expanded into a regional network. Because the plan failed to fall within these rather narrow limits of acceptability, it was defeated.

The 1965 plan, on the other hand, met the congressional requirements on the major points—financing, organization, and destination orientation. In essence, the more incremental plan (1965) had little difficulty in securing congressional approval while the innovative plan (1963) was soundly defeated.

Crisis and the WMATA: 1966-1967[5]

During 1966, the NCTA was engaged in engineering studies for the adopted twenty-five mile system. It was fully expected that by the summer Congress would make funds available for right-of-way acquisition so that actual construction could begin. Congressman William Natcher (D-Ky.), Chairman of the House Appropriations Subcommittee for the District of Columbia, frustrated this hope. His position is explained in the following editorial from the *Washington Post*:

Washington's future subway system is once again in the gravest jeopardy, and this time the city had months of forewarning. Congressman Natcher . . . repeatedly let city officials know that the subway could go forward only if the highway program was also going forward. The Planning Commission (NCPC) has continued to delay all major highway construction and now, predictably, Mr. Natcher has deleted the District's share of the subway construction money. The sum is small, but without it the entire project is frozen. Mr. Natcher is in a strong position. For years public officials, including planners, have been preaching that roads and rails must complement each other. Now both systems are blocked by a dogmatic opposition to all urban highways, regardless of design and location. The next series of highway projects will come before the Planning Commission on Thursday. If it fails to clear the pending highway projects at that meeting, it will automatically delay the subway for a period of at least two years.[6]

Freeway opposition came more from the NCPC, the official planning agency for the District, than from the NCTA. Under its new Administrator, Walter J.

McCarter, the NCTA was able to steer clear of the freeway-subway controversy. The real target of Representative Natcher's wrath was the NCPC, but the effect on the subway was the same as if the NCTA had been his target—funds were not going to be made available for the subway until the freeway program progressed.

The NCPC apparently saw the light. In a stormy meeting at which spectators had to be removed, the Commission voted six to four to proceed with the freeway program. A week later, Natcher released the subway funds.

With the funding problem at least temporarily solved, the NCTA turned its attention to expanding the twenty-five mile adopted system into a regional transit network serving the suburbs as well as the District of Columbia.

Expansion of the system to include the suburbs could only be accomplished by interstate compact since parts of Maryland and Virginia, as well as the District, were involved. The major activity of the NCTA in late 1966 and early 1967 became the realization of such an interstate compact.

The legislation introduced[7] called for the creation of a Washington Metropolitan Area Transit Authority (WMATA) to plan, develop, finance, and provide for the operation of regional transit facilities, and to coordinate the operation of all public and privately owned transit facilities to arrive at a truly regional system.[8] Although there was some minor opposition, the compact legislation aroused no great opposition and easily passed both houses of Congress, as well as the legislatures of Maryland, Virginia, and the District of Columbia.

For purposes of this research, two sections of the compact are of substantial interest. The first, section fifty-one, prohibits the WMATA from operating any of the facilities or providing any of the supporting services, i.e. maintenance, on the transit system.[9] The compact, much like the 1965 legislation, specifically required the operation of the rail system by private enterprise.

The second article of interest, eighty-six, gave the WMATA the power to "expand the basic system authorized by the National Capital Transportation Act of 1965 into a regional system. . . ."[10] The effect of this provision was to require the WMATA to accept the twenty-five mile adopted system as a "given" in its regional planning. Only by new legislation could there be any modification of the 1965 system.

On September 30, 1967, the WMATA officially assumed responsibility from the NCTA for completing the basic system, and for planning, constructing, and providing for the operation of a regional transit system. The Federally created NCTA passed out of existence.[c]

---

[c]The effect of transferring responsibility for the system from a Federal agency to an interstate compact group was that the system was now "owned" by the people of the compact area and not by the Federal Government.

**Modification of the Basic
System: 1967**

In July, 1967, Representative Basil Whitener (D-N.C.) introduced H.R. 11395, to amend the twenty-five mile basic system by eliminating the Columbia Heights line and by adding service to the Independence Avenue-southwest Washington, D.C. area. (see Figure 4-2)

The impetus for this change came ostensibly during the hearings on the NCTA's 1966 budgetary requests. At those hearings, members of the House Appropriations Subcommittee on Interior and Related Agencies expressed concern over the reliability and technical sophistication of NCTA patronage and traffic estimates.[11] The subcommittee directed the NCTA to arrange for a patronage study by an outside contractor,[d] which they willingly did because of some doubts of the feasibility of parts of the 1965 plan.[12]

Two significant findings resulted from the study. First, the Columbia Heights route[e] was found to be the weakest of all lines in the system in terms of peak hour patronage,[f] producing an estimated 3,100 passengers per hour instead of the 6,700 originally forecast.[13] This finding made the line economically not feasible and the NCTA recommended its elimination.

Second, the study showed that the NCTA had overestimated the degree to which traffic congestion in downtown would be lessened due to the twenty-five mile system. The expanded Federal employment in southwest Washington, D.C.[g] turned out to be a source of much potential patronage. Under the authorized system, rail users would ride to 12th and G Streets N.W., and then transfer to a bus to complete their trip to the southwest. To serve the estimated patronage an estimated 120 buses would have to be on the streets during rush hours.

The conclusion was obvious, traffic congestion in the downtown area would be worse instead of improved. The recommended change to serve the southwest is shown in Figure 4-2. This change it was argued, would effectively serve the growing Federal and private employment south of Independence Avenue, estimated to be 87,000 by the year 1980. This modification was not an entirely

---

[d]The contract was awarded to Alan M. Voorhees & Associates of Washington, D.C., the same firm that performed the essential studies of the proposed regional system.

[e]The Columbia Heights line was a spur off of the Connecticut Avenue line serving north-central Washington, D.C. via four stations at New Hampshire and Georgia Avenues N.W., Park Road and 14th Street N.W., Columbia Road and 16th Street N.W., and Columbia and Belmont Roads N.W.

[f]Peak hour patronage is customarily defined as the journey to work, i.e., travel between the hours of 7 and 9 A.M. and 4 and 6 P.M.

[g]Southwest Washington, D.C. is or will be the home for the following Federal and private employment: Agriculture (11,000), HUD (5,600), HEW (17,000), DOD (6,400), DOT (9,000), Treasury (3,800), Smithsonian Institution (1,000), NASA (2,400), others, including GSA (12,300), and private (18,800), for a 1980 projected total of 87,000.

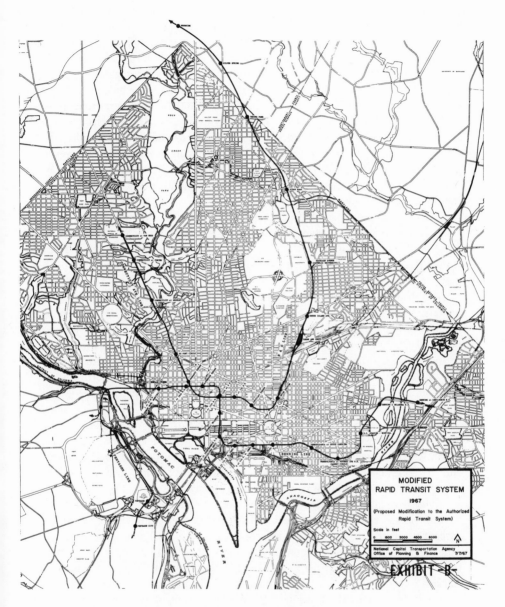

Figure 4–2. Basic System as Modified, 1967.

new proposal as the eighty-three mile system rejected in 1962 included a line to the southwest that was quite similar to the alignment proposed here.

Reaction to the proposed changes was quite favorable during the hearings in both houses. Supporters included eight local governments, one regulatory group, nine planning agencies, two transit companies, and one labor union. The only governmental reservation expressed came from Walter N. Tobriner, President of the Board of Commissioners of the District of Columbia. He expressed concern that the service to north-central Washington, D.C. would not exist unless the Columbia Heights or some alternative route was included in the plan. However, given assurance that some type of rail service between 7th and 14th Streets N.W. was included in the regional plan, the District government supported the modification to the system.

The only real opposition to the elimination of the Columbia Heights line came from citizens and groups of that area. Representatives of the Columbia Heights Business Men's Association, the 18th Street and Columbia Road Business Association, CHANGE Inc. (Columbia Heights Association for Growth and Enrichment), Columbia Heights Citizens Association, and the Adams-Morgan Association, all testified against the proposal. In essence their argument was that denying rail service to north-central Washington, D.C., an area having one of the densest populations, lowest incomes, and lowest car ownership rates in the city, would deprive the people of the inner city of access to jobs.

In addition, its deletion would destroy the potential 20,000 jobs programmed for the area under the region's comprehensive plan for 1985. North-central Washington, D.C., already the site of three ghettos, Shaw, Cardozo, and Adams-Morgan, would inevitably become a slum.

Reaction to the plan came on three general fronts; an attack on the "uneconomic" assumptions of the NCTA, an attack on the Voorhees study which led to the recommendation that the Columbia Heights line be abandoned, and a plea against isolating central city residents from jobs and other opportunities, lest another Watts situation be created.

In its November 1962 report, the NCTA estimated the patronage rates of various income classes of individuals.[h] They found that in low income areas, 88 percent of all travelers would use rail transit where travel times of auto and rail were equal. But even more importantly, even when auto travel was six times faster than rail transit, 76 percent of the low income group would still use rail transit.[14]

A poll taken by local businessmen in the Cardozo area showed that at least 74 percent of those polled would use the Columbia Heights line five or more times

---

[h]Technically this process is called a "modal split" analysis and is used to forecast the proportion of various groups in the population that will use rail transit, buses, automobiles, or some other transit mode under certain conditions.

per week, and only 5 percent would never use the subway.[15] These two findings, according to the supporters of the Columbia Heights line, cast doubt on the assumptions of the NCTA that the line would not generate sufficient patronage to justify itself economically, and that area residents would receive adequate transportation from buses. It was also argued that the Voorhees study was biased against the Columbia Heights line since it was based on providing service only one-half as often as on the rest of the system.

According to opponents of the change, if a person has to wait twice as long as anyone else for a train, he will be less likely to use the service regardless of where he lives. It must be pointed out however, that any bias in this regard originated because of the type of transit line serving the area, and is not due to any bias on the part of the report. As Figure 4-3 points out, the Columbia Heights line is a spur or branch line.

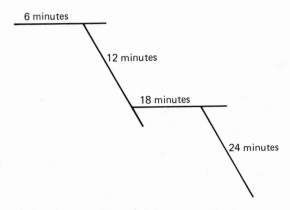

Figure 4–3. Frequency of Service on a Branch Line.

Assuming that service on the main line is to be at six minute intervals, and assuming that equal service is to be provided on the branch line and the main line after branching, then in no case can service be provided to the branch line or the main line at less than twelve minute intervals. By changing the assumption of equal service to one of only every third train going to the branch line, the time between trains becomes eighteen minutes.

More important than the branching problem is the whole nature of ghetto travel. The Voorhees report based its findings on a comparison of rush hour traffic only. But the area served by the Columbia Heights line, according to area residents, has a higher proportion of non-rush hour traffic than the rest of the city because of the low income shift workers who must travel at night.[16]

In a low income area with many people working shift or night work, there are fewer people who travel during the normal peak hours because there are not as many working the normal nine-to-five day. Because of the nature of the employment, there is a wide spread in shifts. Hence, while there may be only 900 people using the rail system at 8 A.M., there may be 700 using it at midnight.[17]

Columbia Heights groups argued that the closing of the system at night when many low income workers would be using it, and eliminating the line entirely, especially when the 1962 NCTA report called for the Columbia Heights-Anacostia line to be built first,[18] clearly showed that the NCTA had no understanding or concern for the problems or needs of ghetto residents.

Finally, the statement of the McCone Commission that the lack of adequate transportation handicapped Watts area residents in seeking jobs and meeting other needs, prompted the following question by George F. Bason, a resident of Columbia Heights:

will despair and frustration lead to rioting in the District of Columbia when the ghetto residents ... see with their own eyes the plush, air-conditioned subways ... for commuters to commute once into and once out of the city every day, while they themselves have not one subway line to serve all their transportation needs throughout the day.[19]

The position of the Columbia Heights groups perhaps can best be summarized by the following quote from the testimony of Chauncey Thomas of CHANGE Inc.:

It seems clear to us either that your entire planning staff is incompetent, or your junking of our subway line was done for political reasons that are not justified in terms of planning for the general public and the interests of the public.

Traditionally, the use of public funds for a transportation system has been justified on the grounds that mass transit benefits blue-collared groups who otherwise could not afford transportation to employment or shopping centers. This is especially valid in this area, where racial segregation in housing prohibits many workers from living near their jobs. The decision to drop the Columbia Heights line for the southwest line is surely an attempt to misuse public funds by suggesting a subway to benefit white suburbanites who can afford other means of transportation while leaving blue-collar Negro and Spanish residents of upper Cardozo to the mercy of inadequate, inconvenient, and expensive bus service.[20]

Richard Severo, author of "Potomac Watch" in the *Washington Post* put all the arguments together quite well in delivering a blast at the plans to eliminate the Columbia Heights line in his column of March 15, 1967:

If the poor people who live in rundown areas of center-city Washington are waiting for a subway system to whisk them to jobs downtown or in suburbia, somebody ought to tell them the wait may be a long one.

For the bitter truth of the matter is, there is nothing planned for them in the immediate future. Later on, maybe, but not now.

The first subway line, it has been decided, has to be out mostly white Connecticut Avenue. Not 14th Street. Not 7th Street. Not Georgia Avenue. . . .[21]

Some of the people connected with the National Capital Transportation Agency are known to feel that they never could have got Congress to go along with the subway system, if they had insisted that initial digging start where it is needed most—in predominately Negro areas of Washington. . . .

No matter what happens, Washington remains impressively ingenious in its ability to avoid serving the people who need services the most. (Emphasis added.)

. . . The subway, which was originally designed to serve the urban poor of the District is to be diverted . . . to serve the commuters of the suburban metropolitan area.

Subways, historically, in other cities, are designed to serve all the people.

This will be the only subway in history to serve the classes instead of the masses.[22]

McCarter of the NCTA and his successor Graham of the WMATA in answering congressional inquiries as to the validity of the charges, referred often to the congressional mandate that the system pay its own way. The following exchange between McCarter and Rep. Whitener is illustrative:

Whitener: Mr. McCarter, the testimony that you have given today . . . would indicate that your decisions are being made on the basis of the intent of Congress that this system be self-sustaining as nearly as possible and that the fare box shall carry the cost of the system.

McCarter: I have taken that as my charge, yes.

Whitener: And so, while we may make arguments about desirability from the individual's point of view of having service to his own community, I take it that you feel that you have no authority to be governed by that type of consideration.

McCarter: . . . I feel that I have no alternative as a professional other than to make this recommendation. . . .

Whitener: . . . we probably were able to sell it (to Congress) because of the engineering studies . . . and the projections which indicated that with the grants of the local and Federal governments that there could be a pay-out of the fare box in a 40 year period.

McCarter: Yes.

Whitener: If we get away from that concept then it seems to me that we are getting into trouble and maybe running the risk of having no system at all.[23]

Aided by the unanimous support of both District Committees, the modified plan easily passed both Houses. It was only in the House that any mention was made of the realities of the problems in urban ghettos and of the frustrations that led to Watts, Detroit, and Newark:

While the statistics presented by the Washington Metropolitan Area Transit Authority in support of its proposal seem persuasive, the fact remains that there will now be no subway route servicing the low-income inner city area.

In this time of urban discontent, when one of the chief problems is unemployment among ghetto residents, the unavailability of cheap, convenient mass transportation only aggravates the problem, it seems an inappropriate and impolitic moment to eliminate the one subway line which would serve these people.[24]

Evaluation

This episode again points out the fare-box orientation of the METRO commitment. As presented to the public, the Columbia Heights issue was one of eliminating an "uneconomic" part of the system in order to provide more highly utilized and more profitable service on the rest of the system. As important as the Columbia Heights spur is in the evolution of the financial orientation of the system, the techniques used by Columbia Heights citizens to save "their" transit service are equally significant. The issue in this case is one similar to an issue facing every planning body involved in large scale public projects. Public interest in a project, and the resulting criticisms and suggestions, seldom focus until a critical decision is reached. In this instance residents of the Columbia Heights area were indifferent towards the subway until service to their neighborhoods was about to be eliminated. Throughout the preliminary planning and early hearings, Columbia Heights interests did not provide any kind of positive pressure to keep their subway line.

Thus when the proposal was made to improve cost-benefit ratios by eliminating service to Columbia Heights, it was already too late to gear up to fight the proposal.

Whether or not the elimination of the Columbia Heights spur could have been prevented (or would have ever been proposed) had the residents of the area been white is not entirely clear. Unfortunately, no comparative data are available for the National Capital area. Some evidence (of an opposite nature) is available from the Bay Area Rapid Transit (BART) project which will result in a rail rapid transit system across San Francisco Bay linking the communities of Oakland and San Francisco. According to some observers of the BART situation, when transit officials were planning seriously, local officials and citizens were not listening. When the latter were finally ready to participate, BART officials believed that they had progressed too far with engineering, financing, and planning to make many of the changes wanted by the citizens. In two cases BART concluded that the changes demanded could not financially be made. Debate was long and bitter with the changes finally coming, but only after San Francisco raised an additional $23 million and Berkeley an additional $20 million to pay for the desired changes.[25]

Given the fare-box orientation of METRO it appears that Columbia Heights residents employed the wrong strategy in trying to keep their subway service. A more rewarding approach might have been to document the economic and other benefits to be gained from keeping the Columbia Heights line. Then, Congress would have been forced to choose between competing "expert" findings, a situation in which Columbia Heights forces would have had a fair chance of success. As it was, their appeal was based mainly on social welfare and need arguments, a strategy not calculated to be successful given the fare-box orientation of the system.

A Regional System At Last: 1968

The final phase in our narrative began in October, 1967 with the WMATA Board of Directors approving a Proposed Regional Rapid Rail Transit System (PRS) of 95.6 miles for presentation to the public. The system consisted of the basic twenty-five mile system as modified in 1967, and seven branch lines to serve the Maryland and Virginia suburbs.

In considering various alternatives for the suburban part of the trip, the Voorhees staff operated under the premise that the basic market for rail transit is peak hour use, and that this is the work trip. Thus, for the system to be successful, i.e. operate in the black, it must be oriented to areas of population concentration at one end and concentrated employment on the other.[26]

In addition, the following kinds of questions were asked in discussing the abilities and limitations of rail rapid transit: (1) how far out from downtown will a significant number of people live who must work downtown, (2) how many non-downtown trips can be attracted to rail rapid transit, (3) and what quality of service can be provided to outlying areas using current technology.[27] Finally, how much service can be provided for non-downtown oriented trips. Can rail rapid transit carry a large enough number of people into suburban centers, and is this number large enough to justify extending transit routes beyond a point that downtown patronage alone would justify.[28]

Looking at these questions the Voorhees staff recommended three alternate systems based on previous route planning and projections for future development. All three systems provided essentially similar service to the region, but with each major travel corridor being served differently by each alternative.

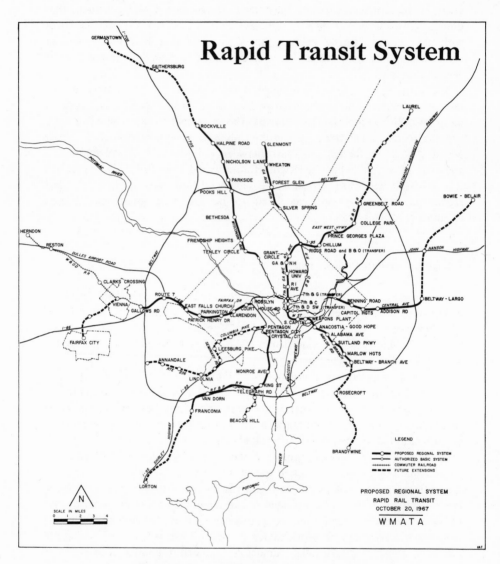

Figure 4–4. Proposed Regional System, 1967.

Although it is not necessary to describe the technology of each system, it might be pointed out that system A consisted of seven radial lines converging on downtown with six lines serving the central city.[i] Alternate B had eight lines with seven of them serving the central city. The essential difference between the two was in the coverage given to eastern and southeastern Prince Georges County, and western and southwestern Fairfax County. System C was different from the other two and was designed to test the effects of commuter rail service on existing tracks in conjunction with the adopted downtown system by merging the two. Figures 4-5 to 4-7 show the three test systems.

The results of the testing process were presented at a series of conferences held in July, 1967 in rural Virginia. Attending the meetings were representatives and staff of local governments in the region, local and regional planning agencies, and state and Federal governments. After two days of meetings and discussions it was agreed that a fourth test system should be analyzed. This alternative included rail transit service in all corridors with several alternate rail alignments within each corridor as possible improvements over the previously tested systems (see Figure 4-8).

The test results of this fourth system were presented at another conference held in Washington, D.C. on October 20. Following a presentation of the findings of the fourth test system, the WMATA staff and officials unanimously recommended the PRS shown in Figure 4-4.

The Proposed Regional System approved by the WMATA reflected political realities in the region as well as planning and technical considerations. Comparing the PRS with the four test systems it becomes obvious that all route and service changes were made in the suburbs and not in the central city. This occurred for two reasons. First, the city portion of the system was set by law (the 1965 Transportation Act as modified in 1967) and could not be redesigned without the approval of Congress. And in view of the difficulty encountered in getting the basic system approved it was considered politic not to suggest any city changes so early in the game. Second, in order to gain the support of the suburban jurisdictions, WMATA officials agreed to permit each area to decide where rail service was to go in that locality. Eventually, the entire system would have to be voted on by the residents of five of the six suburban jurisdictions before those areas could pledge any funds for the building of the system. Some officials felt that permitting each suburban area to decide where the service was to be located in the jurisdiction would gain additional support from the community and possibly guarantee victory at the polls.

Following the adoption of the PRS in October, a series of public hearings were held in Maryland, Virginia, and the District of Columbia to elicit public

---

[i]The line to Brandywine, Maryland, and the line coming out of Alexandria merged south of the central business district to form one line through downtown.

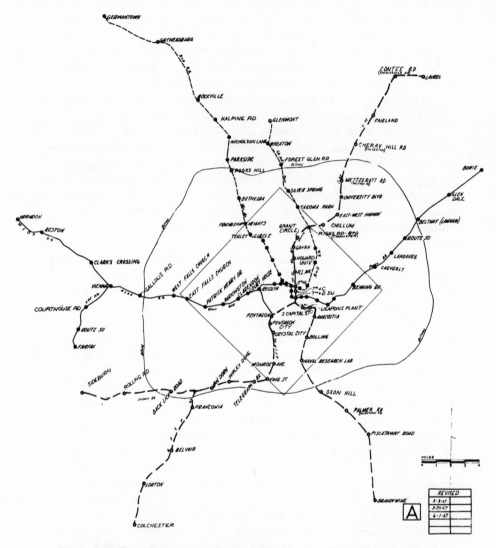

Figure 4–5. Test System A. Source: Washington Metropolitan Area Transit Authority, Office of Engineering.

Figure 4–6. Test System B. Source: Washington Metropolitan Area Transit Authority, Office of Engineering.

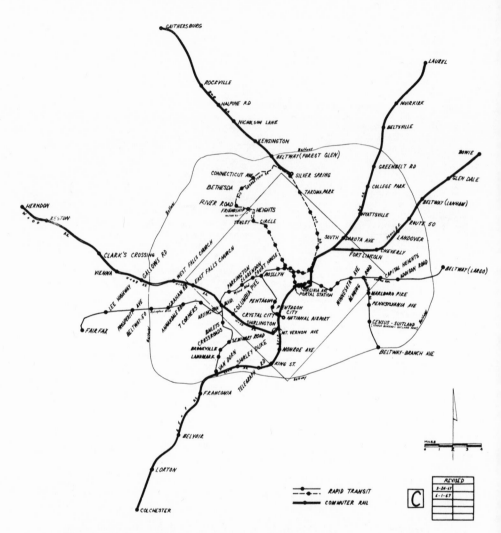

Figure 4–7. Test System C. Source: Washington Metropolitan Area Transit Authority, Office of Engineering.

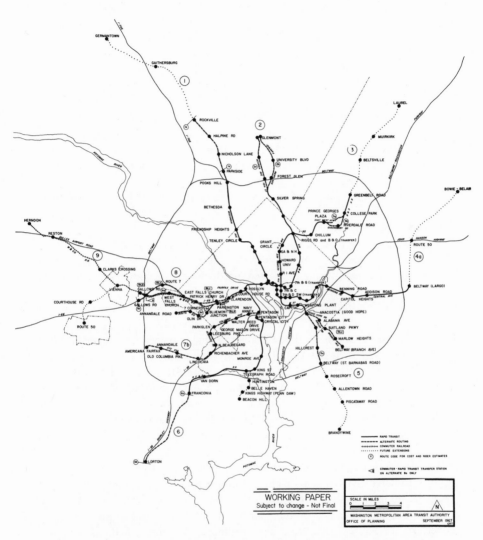

Figure 4–8. Fourth Test System. Source: Washington Metropolitan Area Transit Authority, Office of Planning, Sept, 1967.

response to the system. Two facts are noteworthy in discussing the public hearings on the proposed system. The first is that as in the 1962 plan, the public was presented with a finished document. From all available evidence, it appears that little or no effort was made to involve business, neighborhood, or citizen groups in the planning process. In fact, a planner formerly with Voorhees stated that there was no real citizen participation in the planning process until the PRS was "trotted out." The second item is that the ground rules established for testifying during the hearings were that only people who were residents of the jurisdiction in which the hearings were being held could testify at that hearing. In other words, only District of Columbia residents could testify at District hearings despite the interest of many suburban residents in downtown service. Similarly, no central city resident could testify at a suburban hearing even though he might work or own a business there.

This may appear to be a trivial if not insignificant point, but I would argue that it points to a significant degree of fragmentation in the conception of a nominally regional system.

Throughout its history, the benefits to the entire region, as well as benefits to specific jurisdictions, were touted as the reason for the building of a rail transit system, yet the first time any citizen participation or input was permitted, regional impact and service considerations were ignored.

Although it is difficult to assess the impact of the public hearings, those in the District of Columbia did show some effect, especially a meeting of the 14th Street Merchants Association. The PRS had originally placed the central city line up 7th Street and then out to College Park, Maryland. The system adopted in March, 1968, shifted the central city route to 13th Street after the stop at 7th and G Streets N.W. This change accommodated the demands of the 14th Street group who had complained that the original route would force them out of business. In general though, it was conceded that the District of Columbia hearings were disappointing since most of the people testifying came "straight off of Connecticut Avenue."[29]

Another change involved the Southwest Mall-Benning Road route. Originally planned to serve the Capitol Heights, Addison Road, and Large (Route 495) areas, the adopted system terminated the line at Addison Road, inside Route 495 and created a spur line on the Pennsylvania Railroad right-of-way providing service to Cheverly, Landover, and Ardmore, Maryland, with a possible extension to Bowie.

These changes reflected a decision to serve existing population concentrations thus improving the cost-benefit ratio of the system while ignoring (for the foreseeable future at least) the possibility that METRO could encourage orderly suburban growth in the areas that are currently sparsely populated (Addison Road to Largo). In effect, this change traded off potential orderly suburban growth but lower initial patronage for higher initial patronage levels and more revenue in the fare-box.

The Pentagon-Franconia route in Virginia serving the city of Alexandria also underwent change. Originally the line was to branch at Telegraph Road, south of Alexandria with service continuing along the railroad right-of-way to Franconia. The adopted system, shown in Figure 4-9, retained the branching operation but continued service south one more station to Huntington, and created a spur line before the Franconia terminus to serve Backlick Road and eventually Burke. Finally, the Wilson Boulevard route was rerouted at its western terminus to eliminate service to Vienna, Virginia.

Service to the Huntington area of Alexandria was a non-negotiable demand of that city's participation in the entire regional project. City officials let it be known that unless direct service was provided to the Huntington area, their $30.6 million share of construction costs would not be forthcoming.

The other changes reflected present and future population trends. The addition of a station at Backlick Road took into account the rapidly growing suburban areas in Springfield and North Springfield, Virginia. It also provided rail service to the rural Burke area and to the upper middle class subdivisions of that part of Fairfax County.

Evaluation

With the decision by the NCTA to push for a regional rail transit system, additional congressional constraints on system planning and design became visible. In creating a regional system, the WMATA (NCTA's successor) was required to "expand the basic system authorized by the National Capital Transportation Act of 1965. . . ."[30] To some observers and participants, this requirement was second in importance only to the self-support requirement in impact on the ultimate design and shape of the transit system. What the planners were forced to do was create a regional transportation network out of a downtown oriented twenty-five mile subway.

While such a requirement was not impossible to accomplish from a planning or engineering standpoint, it did affect the ultimate configuration of the lines going from the suburbs into the city. The lines running to Greenbelt and Glenmont, Maryland from the northeast sector of Washington, D.C. and the central city are illustrative of the problem. In several interviews, members of the WMATA planning board said that instead of running a line out the Baltimore and Ohio railroad tracks to Montgomery County, they would have preferred to locate it along Rhode Island Avenue and then out to Prince Georges County. The central city line would then have continued north of the city to Silver

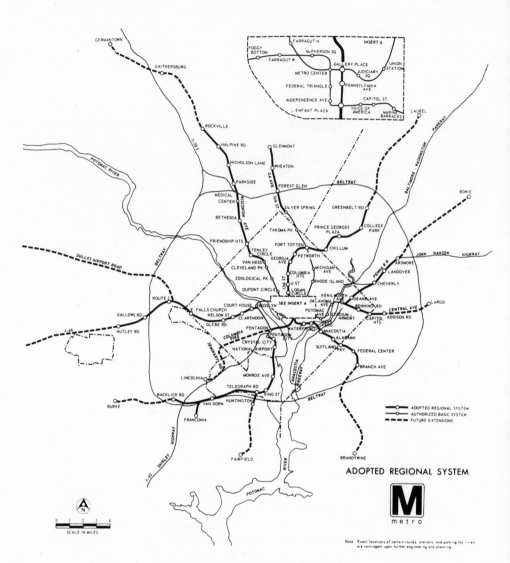

Figure 4-9. Adapted Regional System.

Spring, Wheaton, and Glenmont. Such a change would have accomplished two goals. First, it would have provided direct service to the large low income population residing in northeast Washington, D.C. As it now stands, residents of the area west of the Anacostia River and east of North Capitol Street have very little rail service at their disposal. The second result would have been to provide more direct access to suburban Montgomery County jobs for central city residents. Their trip would have been shorter and no transfer would have been required. Thus from a planning standpoint, the requirement that the twenty-five mile basic system of 1965 be the core of the regional transit network further constrained the WMATA staff in building a regional transit network.

Another group of interests played an important role in the adopting of a regional transit system—the suburbs. Throughout the evolution of the project suburban officials and civic associations had supported the idea of a regional rail system and had exerted considerable effort to get such a system approved. When it became apparent that such a system might become a reality, continued support by the suburbs became a critical requirement of the program.

To assure their continued support, each suburban area was given virtual veto power over the placement and alignment of route within its boundaries. Thus, Alexandria's demand that the Huntington section south of the city be given direct service was written into the plan adopted in 1968. Similarly, Prince Georges County was able to secure the re-routing of the line serving the eastern portion of the County thus assuring service to the white middle class areas of Cheverly and Landover.

From the standpoint of the counties, these changes were necessary in order to win voter approval for over $200 million worth of bond issues. The greater the size of the population to be served by METRO, the better the chances that the voters would approve the bond measures. With the downtown portion of the system already set, the suburbs tried to serve the major population concentrations within their respective counties.

District of Columbia residents came out on the short end of the bargain in this arrangement. With the city portion of the system having been legislated by Congress, and with the suburbs being given virtually a free hand in determining their route structures, city representatives were not able to exert much influence on the configuration of the regional system. The visible result was that intra-city and reverse commuting patterns were given less comprehensive service than were suburb to city commuters.

Part of the explanation as to why Washington, D.C. was not an equal partner in METRO planning has to do with the Federal dominance of the city government and the lack of any elected representative body in the city. From the 1870's until 1967 the government of Washington, D.C. consisted of three presidentially appointed commissioners (two civilians and one from the Army

Engineers) each appointed for three year terms. Under terms of a reorganization that took effect in November, 1967, the Board of Commissioners was replaced by a single commissioner (now called the "Mayor") and a nine member city council, all presidentially appointed.[31]

The new government was given no new functions or powers, nor were any of the relationships between the city and Congress altered. When it came to planning for METRO, it was possible to assign more weight to the demands of the suburbs than to the city because residents of the Nation's Capital were not able to accept or reject whatever system was finally approved. Suburban approval on the other hand was critical for the success of any regional system.[j]

The Freeway Controversy and
Final Approval: 1969

As 1969 came there still had not been one shovelful of dirt turned for the system. The WMATA had proposed, and the public had agreed on a regional rail system, and millions of dollars had been allocated for engineering, planning, and financial studies. But not one dollar had been released for actual construction.

In January, the President submitted his 1970 budget to Congress including $22.9 million for the District's share of METRO construction costs. In June, the Senate by an 84 to 2 vote approved $18.7 million for construction. This item was subsequently deleted in conference committee.

Again, the reason was the city's failure to comply with the 1968 Highway Act and build the Three Sister's Bridge and the North Central Freeway. In 1966, 1968, and again in 1969, Representative Natcher, Chairman of the House Subcommittee on Appropriations for the District of Columbia, refused to allow subway construction funds to be released until the freeway system got underway beyond recall. Although section 23(b) of the Highway Act of 1968 states that:

Not later than 30 days after the enactment of this section the government of the District of Columbia shall commence work on the following projects:

(1) Three Sisters Bridge, . . .
(2) Potomac River Freeway, . . .
(3) Center Leg of the Inner Loop, . . .
(4) East Leg of the Inner Loop, . . .[32]

---

[j]It might be noted that neither the Washington, D.C. Board of Trade, D.C. Transit, the freeway forces, nor other city based groups have the voting franchise in the District of Columbia, yet their interests will be better served by METRO than will those of the inner city resident.

Senators on the D.C. Committee have said that the city is not required to build the Bridge or Freeway while Representatives Natcher and Broyhill have said that construction was the "spirit" of the 1968 act.

On August 9, 1969, the District of Columbia City Council took the first step to resolve the impasse. By a vote of 6 to 2 it reversed a previous stand and authorized a go ahead with the construction of the Three Sisters Bridge and restudy of the North Central Freeway. The meeting however, was not without its problems. Over 200 people attempted to break up the meeting and forced the Council to vote behind barricaded doors.

After the vote it appeared as if the construction funds might finally be released and actual construction could finally begin. But on August 11, Mr. Natcher announced a new condition for the release of the funds: the city must win all lawsuits pending against the Three Sisters Bridge.[33] The reaction of District Officials was immediate and predictable. City Council Chairman Gilbert Hahn, Jr. said he was "disappointed" with Natcher's remarks and that he had been led to believe that the Council's action would secure the release of the subway funds.[34] Council Vice-Chairman Sterling Tucker was more direct; he labeled the statement a "doublecross."[35]

In a surprise move a month later, Natcher announced that he was releasing almost $121 million in METRO funds, including $18.7 million in city funds and $37.4 million in federal contributions.

Although there was no evidence as to why the delay was suddenly ended, a *Washington Post* article noted that Natcher had been under considerable pressure from the White House, members of Congress, and the public to release the subway funds.[36]

An apparent key factor was the decision of the Senate District Committee to keep in the city's pending budget request a rider which would cancel the city's annual Federal contribution if it failed to comply with the provisions of the 1968 Highway Act.[37]

The rest of the evolution proceeded uneventfully. In May, the Secretary of Transportation and the Commissioner of the District of Columbia submitted legislation to Congress authorizing Federal participation in a ninety-seven mile regional system approved by the WMATA (see Figure 4-10). In June, joint hearings were held by the House and Senate District Committees with both committees favorably reporting the legislation. The House vote on November 24, 1969 dramatically overturned the 278 to 76 defeat of the 1963 twenty-three mile plan, as the regional system was passed 285 to 23. Finally, in December, President Nixon signed into law the legislation authorizing federal participation in the regional system, with official ground-breaking ceremonies held on the same day.

METRO Evolved: An Evaluation

As was pointed out in the opening paragraphs of the evolution of METRO, the interests and groups involved in building a subway in the Nation's Capital participated at different times, at different levels of commitment, for different rewards.

Congress, through the Joint Committee on Washington Metropolitan Problems and the House and Senate District Committees, has occupied the most visible, continuous, and important role in the entire process. Congress originally appropriated the money to conduct the Mass Transportation Survey, sponsored the 1958 Lazarus Report critical of the survey's methods, held a full week of public hearings on the 1959 plan, built several important constraints into the 1960 Transportation Act, and defeated a plan in 1963 that would have given the District of Columbia an operational twenty-three mile subway system by 1970. Once certain financial and organizational changes were made in 1965, Congress approved the city's subway. It also gave tacit approval to a regional transit system by passing legislation creating an interstate compact agency to plan a regional transit system. Finally, Congress held up construction funds[k] for the system until the controversial freeway program for the District of Columbia was again underway. For these very obvious and visible reasons then, Congress must be accorded the most important role in the evolution of METRO and in determining its ultimate shape.

The freeway interests and bus companies were also present throughout much of the evolution, each with the same basic goal: to protect their interests and programs. For the highway people the METRO program became a struggle to salvage as much of the 1959 MTS plan as possible, and with the congressional support they received, most notably from Mr. Natcher, they were quite successful. Chalk and his bus company faced a different kind of crisis. In the operating franchise granted to the D.C. Transit Company in 1956, Congress gave the company the exclusive right to operate public transit in the District of Columbia at a guaranteed 6.5 percent annual profit unless legislated otherwise. The goal of the bus company was to become the sole operator of the proposed subway system.

Whether Chalk or some other company will eventually become the operator of METRO, is an unsettled issue. For the past several years the bus company has been facing rising costs and declining revenues to the extent that recent fare increases have pushed the intra-city one-way fare to forty cents. These recent

---

[k]Although it was Representative Natcher who held up the construction funds until late 1969, there was no pressure on him by his colleagues in the House to release the money, so it must be assumed that the House gave at least tacit approval to his refusal to permit any funds for subway construction to be released until the freeway program was underway.

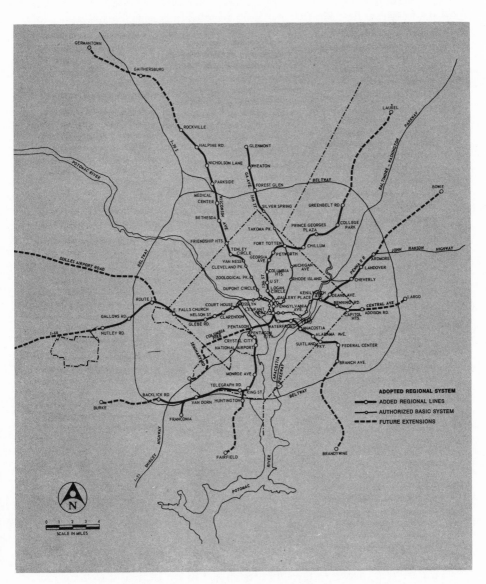

Figure 4-10. Adopted Regional System as Modified, 1969.

increases in the face of growing criticism over declining service levels have led to several proposals for the public takeover of the company. Congress has failed to act on any of the proposals to date, and shows no interest in doing so.

At the local level, the Black United Front (BUF) has called for passengers not to pay more than twenty-five cents for a ride and face arrest to test the legality of the forty-cent fare. The BUF has also attempted to provide free bus service to several ghetto areas in an attempt to force D.C. Transit to lower its fares. Most recently the Rev. Walter Fauntroy, a former Board Chairman of METRO, announced plans to survey bus users in the most heavily traveled inner city areas in order to organize a riders' boycott and bankrupt the company.

However, it is extremely important to note that a private enterprise clause is an essential part of the WMATA compact, and that only transit companies manage transit operations. In other words, the operation of a transit system requires certain expertise regarding routing, schedules, labor provisions, etc. and only those people who are currently in the transit business have this kind of knowledge. Thus, unless WMATA officials are willing or able to establish all the working procedures of METRO and then let a private operator manage the system, it is not unlikely that Chalk will add METRO to his stable of interests.

Significant support for rail transit came from two additional groups, both with substantial support on Capitol Hill, those people interested in preserving the aesthetic values of the area, and the downtown business interests.

Beginning with the 1959 hearings, architectural and environmental spokesmen took every opportunity to convince Congress that rail transit was the only way to meet the region's projected growth and preserve the beauty of the Capitol area. Their message was simple yet forceful: you cannot accommodate the automobile to the extent anticipated in the MTS plan and still keep Washington, D.C. a city of wide boulevards, trees, parks, fountains, and statues. Representative McMillan (D-S.C.) said of David Finley, Chairman of the Fine Arts Commission: ". . . he had dedicated his life to an effort to keep Washington a beautiful city. . . . I know he has no axe to grind. I know he dedicates his life unselfishly to this purpose."[38] With the support of the noted architects Grosvenor Chapman and Victor Gruen, several Congressmen, and editorials in the local newspapers, aesthetic proponents were able to achieve some notable successes.

Downtown business interests were also attracted to rail transit, but for economic reasons. By concentrating service in the downtown area, business representatives saw the subway as revitalizing a physically decaying CBD and recouping some of the sales and revenue that had been lost to the large suburban shopping centers.

The official position of the downtown business community was that rail rapid transit could be a boon to the entire region and to the District of Columbia in particular. Robert Levi, President of the Hecht Company, one of the region's major department stores, noted that "Washington's central business area can only flourish insofar as it is supported by mass transportation connected with the entire metropolitan area."[39] As he continued:

but even possibly more important . . . there must be adequate transportation within the downtown area to permit the efficient, convenient, economical movement and communication of workers and shoppers as they reach the central area.[40]

In a similar vein, O.L. Weir, President of the Washington Metropolitan Board of Trade noted that rail rapid transit:

can constitute a great breakthrough in the economic lethargy which is so prevalent by rejuvenating many business and employment centers including the areas devastated by the riots of 1968.[41]

A downtown orientation for the subway given the constraints imposed by Congress was to be expected. As Levi pointed out, the critical issue for the business people became one of distributing the people throughout the downtown area once they had arrived there.

An examination of METRO's route structure shows that fifteen of the forty-four stations in the District of Columbia will be in the central employment area while eight of the forty-four will be in the central business district.[1] While eight stations may not appear to be a significant number, they are concentrated in approximately a 200 square block area, the very heart of which is METRO Center, the core of the redevelopment and growth expected to occur due to the subway. The eight CBD stations when linked by the proposed feeder bus network will effectively blanket the entire CBD with rapid transit service.

---

[1]The 1959 MTS plan defined the CBD as consisting of that area bounded by 3rd Street N.W. on the east, 20th Street N.W. on the west, Massachusetts Avenue, N.W. on the north, and Constitution Avenue, N.W. on the south.

5 The Policy, Planning, Service Fit

During the several stages of METRO evolution, service-affecting decisions were made that had long term impacts on the entire system. These decisions required choosing from among several sets of policy solutions each with its own anticipated (and unanticipated) policy consequences. In the "classical" decision-making manner such choices would be made using much the following criteria:

(1) faced with a particular problem;
(2) a rational man first clarifies his goals, values, or objectives, and then ranks them in some preference order;
(3) he then lists all the important ways (policies for) achieving his goals;
(4) and investigates all the important consequences that would follow from each of the alternatives and policies;
(5) at which point he is in a position to compare the consequences of each policy with his goals;
(6) and so choose the policy with consequences most nearly matching his goals.[1]

For many and varied reasons this rational man approach to decision making is not entirely applicable to contemporary problem solving.

Issue areas do not segregate themselves into neatly solvable problems. In addition, the pressures of time, financial costs of in-depth analysis, and the inability to foresee the future make it impossible to acquire all the information needed to make a truly rational choice. A third problem arises in ranking goals or values on some kind of hierarchical scale. To the downtown business interests METRO's greatest value is in revitalizing the downtown area thus enabling the business community to recoup some of the business lost to suburban shopping centers. For people who are commuting from the suburbs to downtown, METRO is at its best if it significantly reduces the amount of time needed to get to work. This group may find improved CBD shopping facilities beneficial to them and may even patronize downtown stores with greater frequency than before METRO's construction, but their primary interest in the system is due to its time-saving feature. A third group, those concerned with preserving the aesthetic beauty of Washington, D.C.'s tourist areas, see freeways and highways as a blight on the urban landscape. For these people, METRO is a way to minimize the paving over of much of the city's beauty as well as a way to eliminate much of the auto caused air pollution. Finally, inner city residents view METRO as a means of getting to the suburbs to find jobs and to enjoy the benefits of life in the Nation's Capital.

Several interests, several different and possibly conflicting value preferences, make policy decisions difficult, and according to students of public policy, encourage incrementalism. Relying on the concept of the public interest provides no solutions either, because as Banfield has noted: "no matter how competent and well intentioned, a decision-maker can never make an important decision on grounds that are not in some degree arbitrary or non-logical."[2] He explains that in a complex concrete situation, there is no "ultimate value premise" to which all other values are subordinate. For this reason, the decision-maker must choose from among competing and incompatible solutions, each of which is defensible from some perspective of the public interest.[3]

To deal with this problem, policy makers have developed several strategies for dealing with extremely complex situations. Lindblom outlines seven such strategies (satisficing, bottlenecks, the next change, feedback, remediality, seriality, and incrementalism)[4] of which incrementalism seems to be the most applicable to METRO.

Simply stated, incrementalism means that ". . . what is feasible politically is policy only incrementally or marginally different from existing policies."[5] What this means for METRO is that once Congress had indicated its willingness to accept a rail transit system for the National Capital area, and once a basic system had been approved (1965), subsequent decisions were limited to determining the means for achieving the program, and issues which would have comprehensively reviewed the initial commitment were effectively foreclosed.[6]

Throughout the series of decisions that was to result in METRO, day-to-day decisions and policy were made by two agencies, the Federally created NCTA, and the interstate compact agency, the WMATA. Because of their responsibility to plan, design, and build the METRO system, a complete analysis of the service consequences of the system's planning is impossible without including the role played by the planning agencies themselves.

Conceptually at least, the agencies' role could range from one that is closely controlled by other actors to one of designing a system based on agency created values and priorities.

But as political scientists discovered long ago, few decisions are an either/or proposition. Most, especially complex, expensive, far-reaching decisions, are compromises reflecting political and professional inputs.

At the outset we must note that several of the constraints that the agencies had to live with in planning METRO were established before the creation of the NCTA in 1960. By the time that the Agency began its review of the 1959 MTS plan, it was faced with several significant limitations on its ability to design a regional transit system. Whatever kind of system would eventually be designed would have to be downtown oriented, be capable of being expanded into a regional system, and, most importantly, pay for itself out of the fare-box. Immediately then, constraints established by political actors affected the ability of professionals to act and also affected the ultimate kind of service to be provided.

The 1959 MTS plan also acted as a constraints on the NCTA's freedom to plan a rail rapid transit system; at least to the extent of indicating what was not acceptable. It was obvious that more emphasis had to be given to rail transit than in the MTS plan, but how much more was not known. Nor did the NCTA know how importantly such considerations as the loss of taxable property would be viewed by Congress.

Similar uncertainty surrounded the displacement and relocation of city residents because of the system, and how much disruption of normal business activity would be permitted during METRO construction.

Planning agencies have thus had to choose a course of action based both on their own professional standards and on external goals.[7] As a result, system-affecting decisions have reflected externally imposed constraints, compromises between the needs (values) of various actors, and professional (technical) inputs. During the 1967 debate over the elimination of the Columbia Heights line, inner city residents lost their subway service not only because it was alleged to be uneconomic (a professional decision), but also because their values ran counter to earlier decisions and accepted constraints.

For Banfield, the inability to satisfy all values in a given situation results in a "systematic bias" in the choice of values to be accommodated. In any kind of a complex decision-making situation where there is no ultimate value on which to base a decision, a planner (or planning agency) may be expected to minimize or underrate unconventional, controversial, intangible, or unquantifiable solutions, while favoring those values and solutions that are somewhat conventional, relatively non-controversial, quantative, and factually based.[8]

Similarly, the goals of eliminating discrimination, providing the poor and non-auto owning public with access to jobs and other urban amenities, opening up suburban jobs to inner city residents, and using METRO as a tool of urban redevelopment would receive less sensitive treatment than the goals of relieving traffic congestion, eliminating unnecessary automobiles on the streets, or making money.

All available evidence seems to indicate that these observations are accurate. Beginning with the 1963 hearings on the eighty-three mile regional system and concluding with the 1969 METRO financing hearings, representatives of the planning agencies consistently documented their compliance with externally imposed values and constraints, especially those of Congress, while making no effort to build a case for alternative values or demands.

In defending the 1963 regional system, Warren Quenstedt, Deputy Administrator of the NCTA, took care to point out that:

... initial constructions represents the Agency's compliance at the very outset with the congressional directive that special consideration be given to ... "... early development of a subway from Union Station capable of rapid dispersal of passengers from the railhead to the principal employment centers in the District ...", a subway "...capable of being extended to serve other parts of the region."[9]

Later in the evolution as a regional system was being planned, WMATA decided that the market for rail transit was the home-to-work trip, thus METRO would serve population concentration at one end of the line and employment concentration at the other end. This decision effectively ignored potential subway users whose travel patterns did not fit into the suburb to city pattern.

The planning rationale for this decision was based on the "specialized" nature of rail rapid transit. Such transit, it was argued, is well suited to carrying large numbers of people into an urban center and not well suited for other types of trips.[10] While this decision may have been technically correct, it does point out that rail transit systems usually serve affluent suburban residents and not the bulk of all urban workers.[a]

This instance also illustrates the results of incrementalism failing to lead to a re-examination of basic premises—in this case, who would be served and who should be served.

From the perspective of Banfield's assumptions, several controversy avoiding strategies can be observed on the part of METRO planners. First, there was little effort made to locate potential suburban employment sites and include them in the planning for METRO. This omission more or less accepts the present pattern of development in the region, and assumes much the same kind of growth in the future, despite a nominal dedication to implementing the 1961 "Wedges and Corridors" plan for regional development. Wedges and corridors is a somewhat controversial plan for the year 2000 that proposes to leave greenery and parklike "wedges" as buffer zones between highly developed residential and commercial "corridors."[b]

---

[a]See the quote of Martin Wohl, p. 13 above for greater amplification on this point.

[b]In 1969, Wash.-COG in *The Changing Region, A Comparison of Plans and Policies with Development Trends* (Washington, D.C., 1969), reported that despite a policy level acceptance of the Wedges and Corridors plan, actual implementation had fallen far short of desired levels. Planning for federal employment, housing, and transportation facilities all departed from the plan to keep open wedges between developed corridors. Because of this departure from the goals of wedges and corridors, system planners found it easier to plan METRO accepting present development trends rather than insisting on a strict adherence to wedges and corridors.

In determining route structure, the reverse commuter was given no voice in the planning process while suburban areas were permitted to determine their own service patterns.

The need for financial support from the suburbs in order to build a regional system, and the lack of any ultimate value on which to base route decisions (excluding congressionally legislated values) made it politically easier to permit each suburban jurisdiction to design its own portion of the system so long as fare-box priorities were kept in mind. Several examples of this strategy could be cited but the most apparent is the addition of the Huntington Station south of the city of Alexandria. The Proposed Regional System unveiled early in 1968 terminated service before the Huntington subdivision. Alexandria officials let it be known that without service to that area they would not participate in the plan or contribute to the construction costs. The adopted regional plan of March, 1968 included service to Huntington.

Finally, the fare-box priority established by Congress became a fact of planning. Early in the game it became apparent that to violate this constraint was to have no system at all, a point constantly reinforced in congressional hearings and budgetary sessions. In its simplest form, fare-box considerations determined how and to what extent service questions would be answered.

Not only was the public behavior of the planners controversy or innovation avoiding, the planning documents themselves tend to reinforce these stands and conceal the values and biases underlying the entire planning process.

Thus it is not surprising that nowhere in the official statements of the WMATA do we find an adequate case made for reverse commuting, a coordinated regional transit system (including the buses), or centrally planned regional development changes. While it is unrealistic to expect the WMATA to act as an advocate planner for the poor, in view of Watts, the Kerner Commission Report, public conferences, and general concern over ghetto isolation and the employment problems of inner city residents, it is not unreasonable to expect the WMATA to have presented alternatives to the traditional route structure and service emphasis of METRO. By planning for a homogeneous transportation public the planners glossed over service gaps rather than point out what a conventionally designed system would and would not or even could and could not accomplish.

But what of service? Our analysis has consistently shown that service has generally taken a back seat to financial considerations throughout METRO's evolution. Certain groups in the commuting public, most notably the suburbs to downtown group, will be well served by METRO because their particular travel patterns are those that METRO consciously seeks to meet. Other groups, however, particularly the reverse commuter, will be less satisfied with the level of service METRO will provide.

It is estimated that while 53 percent of suburban Prince Georges County residents who work in the central business district of Washington, D.C. will use METRO to get to work, only 10 percent of the central city residents working in the Maryland suburb will use the rail system.[c] The "why" of the issue lies in the nature of the values that were and were not accommodated in planning the METRO system. Because all the expressed values could not be accommodated in planning and building METRO, the decision-makers had to make choices. Figure 5-1 represents some of the goals (values) at stake in the METRO project.

The pattern of value congruity evident in Figure 5-1 indicates why the less mobile segments of the transportation public (and other innovative goals) will not be benefitted by METRO to the same degree as will other values and interests. Goals (values) above the threshold of change are not compatible with the congressional mandate that the system pay for itself out of the fare-box (minimum appropriated public subsidy) or with the goal of private sector profits,[d] even though they are compatible with all other expressed values in the program.

Serving the reverse commuter falls into this change oriented grouping of values. Any of the values on the "change" side of the diagram would require a substantial public subsidy and would probably not be conducive to maximizing private sector profits. But realizing any (or all) of those values would distribute the benefits from METRO among a much wider segment of the region's population. It has been estimated that if METRO were to own the land immediately surrounding the transit stations (eighty-six of them) the revenues generated from the commercial operations on that land would pay the capital and operating costs of the system, and might allow METRO to operate as a free transit system.[11] This goal is the most change oriented of all those mentioned and is not compatible with the more compelling congressional values. In addition, since such goals are change oriented, their implementation would require innovative action on the part of METRO planners, action that Banfield's hypothesis and our analysis has shown to be incompatible with the external demands placed on the system.

A word of explanation is in order concerning the compatibility between serving the less mobile segment of society and the maintenance of the CBD economy. Theoretically at least, every goal (value) excepting those of profit making and minimal subsidy is compatible with every other goal. Thus, serving the reverse commuter is compatible with maintaining the CBD's economy, with

---

[c]See page 21 above.

---

[d]The legislation creating the WMATA specified that the METRO system would have to be operated by private enterprise. Private profits also include gains from enhanced land values around transit stations, not required by legislation but probably assumed by some members of Congress.

Most-to-Least Status-Quo Conforming

Least-to-Most Status-Quo Conforming	Regional Development Changes	Coordinated Transit System	Service to the Least Mobile	Service to Downtown Rider	Protect Aesthetic Values	Sustain CBD Economy	Minimum Appropriated Public Subsidy	Maximum Private Profit Opportunities
Recapture of Publicly Created Land Values	+	+	+	+	+	+	X	X
Regional Development Changes		+	+	+	+	+	X	X
Coordinated Transit System			+	+	+	+	X	X
Service to the Least Mobile				+	+	+	X	X
Service to the Downtown Rider					+	+	+	+
Protect Aesthetic Values						+	+	+
Sustain Central Business District Economy							+	+
Minimum Appropriated Public Subsidy								+
Maximum Private Profit Opportunities								

Status-Quo Threshold

Change

Figure 5-1. Values in the Metro System.

In the table "X" means that two values are incompatible while "+" indicates that two values are compatible.

preserving the beauty of the capital, and with a regionally coordinated transit system. The incompatibility arises when the external constraints on the system are introduced and when the economic value becomes one of maintaining the dominance of the CBD. Only when a prerequisite of transit service is a downtown orientation supplemented by fare-box considerations and preserving the CBD economy is translated into preserving its dominance in the region, do serving the reverse commuter and preserving the CBD economy become incompatible goals. In the absence of such constraints both goals are equally attainable.

As we have pointed out earlier, system planners have argued that rail rapid transit is at its best when serving a high density core (downtown) and is not particularly well suited to serving other kinds of travel (radial or reverse). Thus in addition to the constraints already mentioned, the practical decision to employ traditional kinds of rail vehicles stacked the deck in favor of certain values and against others.

With the external constraints requiring a CBD orientation, and with a technology geared to serving downtown, values and demands that are supportive of those decisions are more likely to be served than are values which require modification of basic decisions. Certain decisions having been made (the decision that conventional transit vehicles and technology would be used) other kinds of considerations (non-core oriented travel) were no longer open to serious discussion, nor did the decision-making system permit a comprehensive re-examination of basic decisions.

The METRO system as currently planned could be made more adaptable to various transportation needs, including those of the reverse commuter. Such a modification in the service structure would require substantial public subsidies,[e] deviation from congressionally mandated fare-box priorities, and require more central planning and controls[f]—all innovative, controversy producing, status-quo violating policies.

One of the significant findings of the HUD sponsored employment-transportation project in the Watts area of Los Angeles was that even when improvements were made to the bus service in the ghetto there was little noticeable impact in the unemployment level. Project analysts concluded that the diffuse origins and destinations of Watts area residents, and their large amount of off-peak travel made it extremely unlikely that traditional mass transit could meet those travel needs. The Los Angeles experience suggests that a more personal type of transportation would serve the reverse commuter better

---

[e]Extending rail service out past a certain level of population density provides greater service benefits but cannot generate the revenues needed to make such service economically profitable.

---

[f]Instead of permitting each suburban jurisdiction to determine its own service structure.

than traditional mass transit. While the technical attributes of such a system are beyond the scope of this research, it seems that such a system would have to emulate automobile or taxi service in that it is available when a person wants to travel and will take him to (or within walking distance of) his destination. Such a system would provide the reverse commuter with almost door-to-door linking of home and job. However, in no way could this system pay for itself unless fares were so high as to price the service out of the range of the low income reverse commuter. Hence, a technically possible solution is not compatible with a political decision (that the system support itself out of the fare-box).

The policy outcome of all of this is that because change oriented values are not congruent or compatible with certain status-quo values, the less mobile sector of the population does not get served by incremental decision-making in transportation policy.

The "needs," subjective and objective, can be determined. Employment trends and transportation requirements have been given wide attention in governmental and academic circles, yet the service will not be forthcoming.

Thus the statement by Mayor Walter Washington of Washington, D.C. at METRO groundbreaking ceremonies is extremely misleading, but typical of the public relations efforts being made by METRO officials to sell the system to the public. Mayor Washington said that "the same transit cars that whisk suburban commuters in and out of the city will also carry inner-city workers to jobs in nearby suburbs."[12] It is true that in order to maintain the scheduled headways to downtown (two to four minutes in rush hours) trains will have to operate on the same schedule in both downtown and suburban directions. But to imply that the level of service will be comparable between the two destinations is just not true. The very nature of the technology chosen, the values that are going to be served, and the congressionally imposed constraints on the design of the system all preclude this possibility.

Conclusion

The value coalition formed by central business district interests, the suburbs, and aesthetic interests, which when combined with congressionally imposed constraints, foreclosed the possibility of extensive service for Washington, D.C.'s inner city residents. Their interests and needs were not compatible with other expressed values. In addition, the status-quo orientation of the dominant values also contributed to the success of the winning groups. Without exception, the expressed goals of the well-served interests were oriented to "maintenance," "re-vitalization," and "re-building."

On the other hand, service gains for the inner city groups would have required innovative and controversial solutions, an approach Congress, the other groups, and the planners were not prepared to attempt.

From the planning perspective it is ironic that the planners chose to ignore their own-modal-split model developed for the 1962 NCTA report.[g] That report showed that 88 percent of low income people would use rapid transit over autos when travel times for the two modes were equal, while under the same conditions 50 percent of middle income and 32 percent of high income people would use rapid transit.[13] Instead, the planners accepted the constraints imposed by Congress (not surprising in view of Banfield's contention that lacking a politically secure dominant value of their own, planners will adopt external values and goals).

The policy making process to which political scientists have attributed such characteristics as remediality, flexibility, and incrementality, turns out not to be so for groups whose values and needs are not well served by the status-quo. In the METRO episode, the lessons of Newark, Detroit, Los Angeles, and the results of millions of dollars in federally sponsored research seems not to have been learned very well.

Five years after Watts and the McCone Commission findings and two years after the Kerner Commission, a $2.5 billion regional transportation project in the Nation's Capital fails to adequately serve the travel needs of inner city residents.

---

[g]See pp. 72-73 above.

Bibliography

Books

Banfield, Edward C. *Political Influence*. Glencoe: The Free Press, 1961.

Banfield, Edward C. *The Unheavenly City*. Boston: Little, Brown and Company, 1970.

Banfield, Edward C., and Meyerson, Martin. *Politics, Planning, and the Public Interest: The Case of Public Housing in Chicago*. New York: The Free Press of Glencoe, 1955.

Bollens, John C., and Schmandt, Henry J. *The Metropolis, Its People, Politics and Economic Life*. 2d ed. New York: Harper & Row, 1970.

Clark, Kenneth B. *Dark Ghetto: Dilemmas of Social Power*. New York: Harper & Row, 1965.

Hoover, Edgar M., and Vernon, Raymond. *Anatomy of a Metropolis*. New York: Anchor Books, Doubleday & Co., 1962.

Lindblom, Charles E. *The Policy-Making Process*. Englewood Cliffs, N.J.: Prentice Hall, 1968.

Meyer, John R., John F. Kain and Martin Wohl. *The Urban Transportation Problem*. Cambridge, Mass.: Harvard University Press, 1965.

Norling, A.H. *Future U.S. Transportation Needs*. Cambridge, Mass.: United Research Inc., 1963.

Oi, Walter Y., and Shuldiner, Paul W. *An Analysis of Urban Travel Demands*. Evanston, Ill.: Northwestern University Press, 1962.

Owen, Wilfred. *The Metropolitan Transportation Problem*. 2d ed. New York: Anchor Books, Doubleday & Co., 1966.

Pickard, Jerome P. *Dimensions of Metropolitanism*. Research Monograph No. 14. Washington, D.C.: Urban Land Institute, 1967.

Warner, S.L. *Stochastic Choice of Mode in Urban Travel: A Study in Binary Choice*. Evanston, Ill.: Northwestern University Press, 1962.

Articles

Altshuler, Alan. "Transit Subsidies: By Whom, For Whom?" *Journal of the American Institute of Planners*, 35, No. 2 (March, 1969), 84-89.

105

Downs, Anthony. "Alternative Futures for the American Ghetto." *Daedalus*, 97, *The Conscience of the City* (Fall, 1968), 1331-1378.

Downs, Anthony. "The Land-Value Impacts of Transportation Arteries and How They Affect New City Development." *Urban Problems and Prospects*. Ed. Anthony Downs. Chicago: Markham Publishing Company, 1970.

Easton, David. "The New Revolution in Political Science." *American Political Science Review*, 58, (December, 1969), 1051-1061.

Eidenberg, Eugene. "The Presidency: Americanizing the War in Vietnam." *American Political Institutions and Public Policy*. Ed. Allan P. Sindler. Boston: Little, Brown and Company, 1969.

Hirsch, Werner Z. "The Supply of Urban Public Services." *Issues in Urban Economics*. Ed. Harvey S. Perloff and Lowden Wingo, Jr. Baltimore, Md.: The Johns Hopkins Press, for Resources for the Future Inc., 1968.

Kain, John F. "The Distribution and Movement of Jobs and Industry." *The Metropolitan Enigma: Inquiries Into the Nature and Dimensions of America's "Urban Crises."* Ed. James Q. Wilson. Washington, D.C.: U.S. Chamber of Commerce, 1967.

Kain, John F., and Persky, Joseph. "Alternatives to the Gilded Ghetto." *The Public Interest*. No. 14. (Winter, 1969), 74-87.

Kalachek, Edward. "Ghetto Dwellers, Transportation, and Employment." *Interrelationships of Transportation and Poverty: Summary of a Conference on Transportation and Poverty*. Brookline, Mass.: American Academy of Arts and Sciences, 1968.

Lash, Michael. "Case Study: Conflict in Rapid Transit Planning." *Urban Mass Transit Planning*. Ed. Wolfgang S. Homburger. Berkeley, Calif.: University of California, Institute of Transportation and Traffic Engineering, 1967.

McDermott, John, et al. "The Urban Institute View of the Seventies." *Nation's Cities*, 7 (November, 1969), 18-21.

Margolis, Julius. "The Demand for Urban Public Services." *Issues in Urban Economics*. Ed. Harvey S. Perloff and Lowden Wingo, Jr. Baltimore, Md.: The Johns Hopkins Press, for Resources for the Future Inc., 1968.

Meyer, John R. "Urban Transportation." *The Metropolitan Enigma: Inquiries Into the Nature and Dimensions of America's "Urban Crisis."* Ed. James Q. Wilson. Washington, D.C.: U.S. Chamber of Commerce, 1967.

Meyer, John R., and John F. Kain. "Interrelationships of Transportation and Poverty: Summary of a Conference on Transportation and Poverty." *Interrelationships of Transportation and Poverty: Summary of a Conference on Transportation and Poverty*. Brookline, Mass.: American Academy of Arts and Sciences, 1968.

Meyerson, Martin. "Urban Policy: Reforming Reform." *Daedalus*, 97, *The Conscience of the City* (Fall, 1968), 1410-1430.

Moses, L.N., and H.F. Williamson. "Value of Time, Choice of Mode, and the Subsidy Issue in Urban Transportation." *Journal of Political Economy*, 71 (June, 1963), 247-264.

Myers, Sumner. "Personal Transportation for the Poor." *Interrelationships of Transportation and Poverty: Summary of Conference on Transportation and Poverty*. Brookline, Mass.: American Academy of Arts and Sciences, 1968.

Public Documents

Hearings Before the National Commission on Urban Problems, Paul H. Douglas, Chairman. Vol. 5, Detroit, St. Louis, East St. Louis, Washington, D.C., Washington, D.C.: Government Printing Office, 1967.

Highway Act of 1968. Statutes at Large, Vol. 72 (1968).

National Capital Transportation Act of 1960. Statutes at Large, Vol. 74 (1960). *U.S. Code*, Vol. 40 (1960).

U.S. Civil Service Commission. *Annual Report of Federal Civilian Employment in the United States by Geographical Area, 1967*. Washington, D.C.: Government Printing Office, 1969.

U.S. Congress. House. Committee on the District of Columbia. *Amend the National Capital Transportation Act of 1965. Hearings* before Subcommittee No. 4 of the Committee on the District of Columbia, House of Representatives, on H.R. 11395, 90th Cong., 1st Sess., 1967.

U.S. Congress. House. Committee on the District of Columbia. *Mass Transportation in the District of Columbia*. H. Rept. 2751 To Accompany S. 3073, 84th Cong., 2d Sess., 1956.

U.S. Congress. House. Committee on the District of Columbia. *Transit Development Program for the National Capital Region*. H. Rept. 1005 To Accompany H.R. 8929, 88th Cong., 1st Sess., 1963.

U.S. Congress. House. Committee on the District of Columbia. *Transit Program for the National Capital Region. Hearings* before Subcommittee No. 6 of the Committee on the District of Columbia. House of Representatives, on H.R. 6633 and H.R. 7240, 88th Cong., 1st Sess., 1963.

U.S. Congress. House. Representative Bingham speaking against amending the National Capital Transportation Act of 1965. H.R. 11395, 90th Cong., 1st Sess., Oct. 9, 1967. *Congressional Record*, 113, 28156.

U.S. Congress. House. 88th Cong., 1st Sess., Dec. 9, 1963. *Congressional Record*, 109, 23872.

U.S. Congress. House and Senate. *Financing Subway System for the National Capital Region. Hearings* Before the Committee on the District of Columbia and Subcommittee No. 4 of the Committee on the District of Columbia. Congress of the United States, on S. 2185 and H.R. 11191. 91st Cong., 1st Sess., 1969.

U.S. Congress. Joint Committee on Washington Metropolitan Problems. *Metropolitan Transportation* by Arthur Lazarus. Joint Committee Print. Washington, D.C. Government Printing Office, 1958.

U.S. Congress. Joint Committee on Washington Metropolitan Problems. *Transportation Plan for the National Capital Region. Hearings* before the Joint Committee on Washington Metropolitan Problems, Congress of the United States. 86th Cong., 1st Sess., 1959.

U.S. Congress. Senate. Committee on the District of Columbia. *General Information Relating to the Committee on the District of Columbia Together with the Origin and Form of the Government of the District of Columbia.* Committee Print. 91st Cong., 1st Sess., 1969.

U.S. Congress. Senate. Committee on the District of Columbia. *Public Opinion in Washington, D.C. Regarding New Freeways* by Oliver Quayle. 91st Cong., 1st Sess. Washington, D.C.: Government Printing Office, 1969.

U.S. Congress. Senate. Committee on the District of Columbia. *Transportation for the National Capital Region.* S. Rept. 1631 To Accompany H.R. 11135, 86th Cong., 2d Sess., 1960.

U.S. Congress. Senate. Committee on the Judiciary. *Washington Metropolitan Area Transit Authority Compact. Hearings* before a Special Subcommittee of the Committee on the Judiciary, Senate, on S. 3488, 89th Cong., 2d Sess., 1966.

U.S. Congress. Senate. *To Provide for Public Ownership of the Mass Transit Bus System Operated by D.C. Transit System.* S. 1814, 91st Cong., 1st Sess., 1969.

U.S. Department of Commerce. Bureau of the Census. *Census of Business: 1954, 1958, 1963.* Vol. 2, *Retail Trade.* Area Statistics, District of Columbia, Maryland, Virginia.

U.S. Department of Commerce. Bureau of the Census. *Census of Business: 1954, 1958, 1963.* Vol. 4, *Wholesale Trade.* Area Statistics, District of Columbia, Maryland, Virginia.

U.S. Department of Commerce. Bureau of the Census. *Census of Business: 1967. Retail Trade.* Area Statistics (preprint), District of Columbia, Maryland, Virginia.

U.S. Department of Commerce. Bureau of the Census. *Census of Business: 1967. Wholesale Trade*. Area Statistics (preprint), District of Columbia, Maryland, Virginia.

U.S. Department of Commerce. Bureau of the Census. *Census of Manufactures: 1954, 1958, 1963*. Vol. 3, Area Statistics, District of Columbia, Maryland, Virginia.

U.S. Department of Commerce. Bureau of the Census. *Consumer Income*. Series P-60, Table 48, April, 1966.

U.S. Department of Commerce. Bureau of the Census. *County Business Patterns: 1953, 1959, 1962, 1967*. Pts. 1, 2, & 3, District of Columbia, Maryland, Virginia.

U.S. Department of Commerce. Bureau of the Census. *United States Census of Population: 1950 and 1960*. Vol. I, Characteristics of the Population, Pt. 10, District of Columbia, Pt. 22, Maryland, Pt. 48, Virginia.

U.S. Department of Commerce. Bureau of the Census. *United States Census of Population: 1960. Place of Work and Means of Transportation to Work*. Supplementary Report.

U.S. Department of Commerce. Bureau of the Census. *United States Census of Population: 1960*. Vol. 2, *Journey to Work*.

U.S. Department of Commerce. Bureau of the Census. *United States Census of Population: 1970. Population Count for Standard Metropolitan Statistical Areas*, Preliminary Report.

U.S. Department of Housing and Urban Development. *A Profile of Suburbs and Central Cities in the United States*. Fifth Draft. Unpublished Report, August, 1968.

U.S. Department of Housing and Urban Development. Office of Metropolitan Development. Urban Transportation Administration. *Tomorrow's Transportation, New Systems for the Urban Future*. Washington, D.C.: Government Printing Office, 1968.

U.S. Department of Labor. Bureau of Labor Statistics. *Recent Trends in Social and Economic Conditions of Negroes in the United States*. Current Population Reports. Series P-23, No. 26, BLS Report No. 347. Washington, D.C.: Government Printing Office, July, 1968.

U.S. Department of Labor. Bureau of Labor Statistics. *Three Standards of Living for An Urban Family of Four Persons*. Bulletin No. 1570-1575. Washington, D.C.: Government Printing Office, 1969.

Reports

Banks, Robert L. "The Legislative Origins of the National Capital Transportation Agency." Discussion paper for the NCTA Conference sponsored by the Washington Center for Metropolitan Studies, Annapolis, Md., October, 1961.

Development Research Associates. *Benefits to the Washington Area from the Adopted Regional METRO System. Technical Appendix.* Washington, D.C., 1968.

Ganz, Alexander. *Emerging Patterns of Urban Growth and Travel.* M.I.T. Project Transport. Cambridge, Mass.: Massachusetts Institute of Technology, 1968.

Metropolitan Washington Council of Governments. *Metropolitan Area Statistics, 1968.* Washington, D.C., 1969.

Morris, Robert L. *Preliminary Regional System Planning Report.* Presented to the WMATA Board of Directors, Washington, D.C., February, 1967. Washington, D.C.: Office of Planning and Finance, WMATA, 1967.

National Capital Transportation Agency. *Appendix to the November, 1962 Report to the President.* Vol. 5, *System Planning.* Washington, D.C.: Government Printing Office, 1963.

National Capital Transportation Agency. *Rail Rapid Transit for the Nation's Capital—Transit Development Program, 1965.* Washington, D.C.: Government Printing Office, 1965.

National Capital Transportation Agency. *Transportation in the National Capital Region—Finance and Organization.* Washington, D.C.: Government Printing Office, 1962.

Plavnik, Robert L. *The Washington Metropolitan Area—Population and Employment.* Presented to the WMATA Board of Directors, Washington, D.C., February, 1967. Washington, D.C.: Office of Planning and Finance, WMATA, 1967.

Pratt, Richard H. *Considerations in Rail Rapid Transit Planning.* Presented to the WMATA Board of Directors, Washington, D.C., February, 1967. Washington, D.C.: Office of Planning and Finance, WMATA, 1967.

Report of the National Advisory Commission on Civil Disorders. Otto Kerner, chairman. New York: Bantam Books, 1968.

Smith, Larry & Company. *Use of Excess Land and Air Rights.* Prepared for the National Capital Transportation Agency. Washington, D.C., 1962.

Smith, Wilbur & Associates. *Maryland Capital Beltway Impact Study.* Final Report. New Haven, Conn.: Wilbur Smith and Associates, 1968.

Smith, Wilbur & Associates. *Mass Transportation Survey. Traffic Engineering Study*. New Haven, Conn.: Wilbur Smith and Associates, 1959.

Transportation Research Institute, Carnegie-Mellon University. *Latent Demand for Urban Transportation*. Washington, D.C.: U.S. Department of Housing and Urban Development, 1968.

U.S. National Capital Planning Commission and U.S. National Capital Regional Planning Council. *Report of the Joint Committee on Program and Procedures*. Washington, D.C., June 16, 1955.

U.S. National Capital Planning Commission and U.S. National Capital Regional Planning Council. *Transportation Plan for the National Capital Region: The Mass Transportation Survey Report–1959*. Washington, D.C.: Government Printing Office, 1959.

U.S. National Capital Planning Commission. Mass Transportation Survey, Joint Steering Committee. *Transcript of Proceedings, July Meeting*. Washington, D.C., July 8, 1958.

Violence in the City–An End or a Beginning, a Report by the Governor's Commission on the Los Angeles Riots. John A. McCone, chairman. Los Angeles, Calif., 1965.

Voorhees, Alan M. & Associates. *Washington Area 1980 Rail Rapid Transit Forecast*. Prepared for the National Capital Transportation Agency. McLean, Va., 1967.

Washington Metropolitan Area Transit Authority. *METRO Ridership*. News Release. Washington, D.C.: WMATA, December, 1969.

Washington Metropolitan Area Transit Authority. *Traffic Forecast*. Prepared by Alan M. Voorhees & Associates. Technical Report No. 3. Washington, D.C.: WMATA, 1967.

Newspapers

Sunday Star. Editorial, July 12, 1959.

Washington Post and Times Herald. Editorial, July 12, 1959, Editorial, October 12, 1959, Editorial, December 11, 1963, Editorial, September 10, 1966.

Washington Post and Times Herald. December 14, 1967, January 7, 1968, August 12, September 25, 1969.

Washington Post and Times Herald. "The Federal Diary." by Mike Causey. May 17, 1970.

Washington Post and Times Herald. "Lessons for METRO from San Francisco." By James E. Clayton. January 11, 1970.

Washington Post and Times Herald. "Potomac Watch." By Richard Severo. March 15, 1967.

Interviews and Speeches

Hanson, Royce. President of the Washington Center for Metropolitan Studies. Statement before the open meeting of the D.C. Advisory Committee of the U.S. Commission on Civil Rights. Washington, D.C., May 14, 1970. (Typewritten).

Hechinger, John. Former Chairman, District of Columbia City Council. Statement before the open meeting of the D.C. Advisory Committee of the U.S. Commission on Civil Rights. Washington, D.C., May 14, 1970. (Typewritten).

Pratt, Richard H. Private Interview in Bethesda, Md., January 2, 1970.

Washington, Walter. Mayor of Washington, D.C. Remarks at METRO Ground-breaking Ceremonies. December 9, 1969. (Mimeographed).

Other

Automobile Manufacturing Association. *1968 Automobile Facts and Figures.*

Metropolitan Washington Council of Governments. Transportation Planning Board. *Home Interview Survey.* Washington, D.C., 1968. (Computer Tape).

Notes

Notes to Chapter 1

1. Wilfred Owen, *The Metropolitan Transportation Problem* (2d ed.; New York: Anchor Books, Doubleday and Company, 1966).

2. Ibid., p. 7.

3. Arguments for making urban services more client- and user-oriented can be found in Martin Meyerson, "Urban Politics: Reforming Reform," 97, *Daedalus, The Conscience of the City* (Fall, 1968); Werner Z. Hirsch, "The Supply of Urban Public Services," and Julius Margolis, "The Demand for Urban Public Services," both in *Issues in Urban Economics*, ed. Harvey S. Perloff and Lowden Wingo, Jr. (Baltimore, Md.: The Johns Hopkins Press, for Resources for the Future Inc., 1968).

4. Also see pp. 13-14 and 47.

5. *Violence in the City—An End or a Beginning, A Report by the Governor's Commission on the Los Angeles Riots*, John A. McCone, chairman (Los Angeles, California: December 2, 1965), p. 65.

6. Ibid., p. 38.

7. John F. Kain and Joseph Persky, in "Alternatives to the Gilded Ghetto," *The Public Interest*, No. 14 (Winter, 1969), pp. 75-77, report that when black and white residential locations are compared for the suburbs of the ten largest metropolitan areas, whites at all income levels are much more suburbanized than are blacks at the same income level.

8. John R. Meyer, John F. Kain, and Martin Wohl, *The Urban Transportation Problem* (Cambridge, Mass.: Harvard University Press, 1965), p. 54.

9. John F. Kain, "The Distribution and Movement of Jobs and Industry," in *The Metropolitan Enigma: Inquiries Into the Nature and Dimensions of America's "Urban Crisis,"* ed. James Q. Wilson (Washington, D.C.: U.S. Chamber of Commerce, 1967), p. 11.

10. Wilber Smith and Associates, *Maryland Capital Beltway Impact Study, Final Report* (New Haven, Conn.: Wilbur Smith and Associates, 1968), p. 11.

11. U.S. Department of Commerce, Bureau of the Census, *United States Census of Population: 1950 and 1960*, Vol. 1, *Characteristics of the Population; United States Census of Population: 1970*, preliminary report, *Population Count for Standard Metropolitan Statistical Areas*; and Metropolitan Washington Council of Governments, *Metropolitan Area Statistics, 1968*.

12. The original forecast of the decline in importance of the central city as a place of employment was by Edgar M. Hoover and Raymond Vernon, *Anatomy*

of a Metropolis (New York: Anchor Books, Doubleday and Company, 1962). More recently, Edward C. Banfield has reiterated these trends in his *The Unheavenly City* (Boston: Little, Brown and Company, 1970), pp. 34-35.

13. For elaboration on this point, see Hoover and Vernon, *Anatomy of A Metropolis*, pp. 85-86 and 97.

14. Mike Causey, "The Federal Diary," *Washington Post and Times Herald*, May 17, 1970.

15. Ibid.

16. Royce Hanson, President, Washington Center for Metropolitan Studies, statement before the open meeting of the D.C. Advisory Committee of the U.S. Commission on Civil Rights, May 14, 1970.

17. John Hechinger, former Chairman, District of Columbia, City Council, statement before the open meeting of the D.C. Advisory Committee of the U.S. Commission on Civil Rights, May 14, 1970.

18. Hoover and Vernon, *Anatomy of A Metropolis*.

19. Kain, "Distribution and Movement of Jobs."

20. John R. Meyer, "Urban Transportation," in *The Metropolitan Enigma: Inquiries Into the Nature and Dimensions of America's "Urban Crisis"*, ed. James Q. Wilson (Washington, D.C.: U.S. Chamber of Commerce, 1967), p. 39.

21. John C. Bollens and Henry J. Schmandt, *The Metropolis, Its People, Politics, and Economic Life* (2d ed.; New York: Harper & Row, 1970), p. 168.

22. *U.S. Census of Population: 1960*, Vol. 1, *Characteristics of the Population*, pt. 10, District of Columbia, and Oliver Quayle, *Public Opinion in Washington, D.C. Regarding New Freeways*, compiled for the Committee on the District of Columbia, Senate, 91st Cong., 1st Sess., 1969, p. 9.

23. Jerome P. Pickard, *Dimensions of Metropolitanism*, Research Monograph No. 14 (Washington, D.C.: Urban Land Institute, 1967), p. 19.

24. Alexander Ganz, *Emerging Patterns of Urban Growth and Travel*, M.I.T. Project Transport (Cambridge, Mass.: Massachusetts Institute of Technology, 1968), p. 3.

25. Ibid.

26. U.S. Department of Housing and Urban Development, Office of Metropolitan Development, Urban Transportation Administration, *Tomorrow's Transportation, New Systems for the Urban Future* (Washington, D.C.: U.S. Government Printing Office, 1968), p. 13.

27. Automobile Manufacturing Association, *1968 Automobile Facts and Figures*, p. 45.

28. HUD, *Tomorrow's Transportation*, p. 16.

29. Alan Altshuler, "Transit Subsidies: By Whom, For Whom?" *Journal of the American Institute of Planners*, 35, No. 2 (March, 1969), 84.

30. Anthony Downs in "Alternative Futures for the American Ghetto," *Daedalus*, 97, *The Conscience of the City* (Fall, 1968), 1333, notes that there is not a single significant government program aimed at altering the continued concentration of non-whites in the central city, nor are there likely to be any unintended results in this direction.

31. Kain and Persky, "Alternatives to the Gilded Ghetto."

32. Kenneth B. Clark, *Dark Ghetto: Dilemmas of Social Power* (New York: Harper & Row, 1965).

33. Transportation Research Institute, Carnegie-Mellon University, *Latent Demand for Urban Transportation* (Washington, D.C.: U.S. Department of Housing and Urban Development, 1968), pp. 63-64.

34. Transportation Research Institute, *Latent Demand*, p. 10.

35. Altshuler, "Transit Subsidies," 85.

36. John McDermott, et al. "The Urban Institute View of the Seventies," *Nation's Cities*, 7 (November, 1969), 21.

37. Meyerson, "Urban Policy: Reforming Reform," 1415.

38. Edward C. Banfield, *Political Influence* (Glencoe, Ill.: The Free Press, 1961), pp. 330-331.

Notes to Chapter 2

1. See John R. Meyer, John F. Kain, and Martin Wohl, *The Urban Transportation Problem* (Cambridge, Mass.: Harvard University Press, 1965); Transportation Research Institute, Carnegie-Mellon University, *Latent Demand for Urban Transportation* (Washington, D.C.: U.S. Department of Housing and Urban Development, 1968); and Walter Y. Oi and Paul W. Shuldiner, *An Analysis of Urban Travel Demands* (Evanston, Ill.. Northwestern University Press, 1962).

2. Automobile Manufacturing Association, *1968 Automobile Facts and Figures*, p. 45.

3. Oliver Quayle, *A Survey of Public Opinion in Washington, D.C. Regarding New Freeways*, compiled for the Committee on the District of Columbia, United States Senate, 91st Cong., 1st Sess., p. 9.

4. Washington Metropolitan Area Transit Authority, *Traffic Forecast*, Technical Report No. 3, prepared by Alan M. Voorhees & Associates (Washington, D.C.: WMATA, 1967), p. 53.

5. For a detailed explanation of price elasticity and the choice of mode, see Oi and Shuldiner, *Urban Travel Demands*; S.L. Warner, *Stochastic Choice of Mode in Urban Travel: A Study in Binary Choice* (Evanston, Ill.: Northwestern University Press, 1962); and L.N. Moses and H.F. Williamson, "Value of Time, Choice of Mode, and the Subsidy Issue in Urban Transportation," *Journal of Political Economy*, 71 (June, 1963), 247-264.

6. A.H. Norling, *Future United States Transportation Needs* (Cambridge, Mass.: United Research Inc., 1963), V-45.

7. In a briefing session before the Montgomery County Council on December 13, 1967, Mr. Richard Pratt of the Voorhees company (one of the major system consultants to the WMATA) said that METRO will not be a major means of carrying District residents to jobs in Montgomery County. Voorhees figures showed that only 7,000 Washington, D.C. residents working in the County would use the subway. *Washington Post and Times Herald*, December 14, 1967, p. B-2.

8. WMATA, *Traffic Forecast*, p. 81.

9. Robert L. Plavnik in *The Washington Metropolitan Area—Population and Employment*, summary of a presentation to the Washington Metropolitan Area Transit Authority (Washington, D.C.: Office of Planning and Finance, WMATA, 1967), p. 9, has estimated that there are more than 175,000 jobs in the corridor between Rosslyn and the Pentagon.

10. *METRO Ridership* (Washington, D.C.: WMATA, December, 1969), p. 1.

11. Alan M. Voorhees & Associates, *Washington Area 1980 Rail Rapid Transit Patronage Forecast* (McLean, Va.: July, 1967), p. 76.

12. Ibid., pp. 76-77.

13. Ibid., p. 78.

14. Ibid.

15. U.S. Congress, Senate, *To Provide for the Public Ownership of the Mass Transit Bus Sytem Operated by D.C. Transit System*, S. 1814, 91st Cong., 1st Sess., 1969, Sec. 2(2).

16. Development Research Associates, *Benefits to the Washington Area from the Adopted Regional Metro System*, Technical Appendix (Washington, D.C., 1968), p. 4.

17. Quayle, *Public Opinion on New Freeways*, p. 20.

18. *Washington Post and Times Herald*, January 7, 1968, p. C-1.

19. Ibid.

20. Sumner Myers, "Personal Transportation for the Poor," *Interrelationships of Transportation and Poverty: Summary of Conference on Transportation and Poverty* (Brookline, Mass.: American Academy of Arts and Sciences, 1968), p. 7.

21. Ibid.

22. Ibid.

23. Ibid.

24. U.S. Department of Labor, Bureau of Labor Statistics, *Three Standards of Living for an Urban Family of Four Persons* (Washington, D.C.: U.S. Government Printing Office, 1969). Since these data were published, prices have risen at least another 6 percent which probably raises the standard another $500.

25. Ibid.

26. Quayle, *Public Opinion on New Freeways*, p. 8.

27. Ibid., p. 9.

28. U.S. Department of Labor, Bureau of Labor Statistics, *Recent Trends in Social and Economic Conditions of Negroes in the United States*, Current Population Reports, Series P-23, No. 26, BLS Report No. 347 (Washington, D.C.: Government Printing Office, July, 1968), p. 16.

29. Ibid.

30. Quayle, *Public Opinion on New Freeways*, p. 8.

31. See the *Report of the National Advisory Commission on Civil Disorders*, Otto Kerner, chairman (New York: Bantam Books, 1968), p. 392; *Violence in the City—An End or a Beginning, A Report by the Governor's Commission on the Los Angeles Riots*, John A. McCone, chairman (Los Angeles, California, 1965), pp. 65 and 83; Edward Kalachek, "Ghetto Dwellers, Transportation, and Employment," and John R. Meyer and John F. Kain, "Inter-relationships of Transportation and Poverty: Summary of a Conference on Transportation and Poverty," both in *Interrelationships of Transportation and Poverty: Summary of Conference on Transportation and Poverty* (Brookline, Mass.: American Academy of Arts and Sciences, 1968).

32. *Hearings Before the National Commission on Urban Problems*, Paul H. Douglas, chairman, Vol. 5, Detroit, St. Louis, East St. Louis, Washington, D.C. (Washington, D.C.: Government Printing Office, 1967), p. 366.

33. Quayle, *Public Opinion on New Freeways*, p. 10.

34. Ibid.

35. Ibid., p. 23.

36. Ibid., p. 20.

Notes to Chapter 3

1. Martin Meyerson and Edward C. Banfield, *Politics, Planning, and the Public Interest; the Case of Public Housing in Chicago* (New York: The Free Press of Glencoe, 1955), p. 269.

118

2. Ibid.

3. Ibid.

4. Robert L. Banks, "The Legislative Origins of the National Capital Transportation Agency," Discussion paper for the NCTA conference sponsored by the Washington Center for Metropolitan Studies (Annapolis, Md., October, 1961).

5. *Second Supplemental Appropriations Act of 1955, Statues at Large*, 69, 33 (1961).

6. Ibid.

7. National Capital Planning Council and National Capital Regional Planning Council, *Report of the Joint Committee on Program and Procedures* (June 16, 1955).

8. U.S. Congress, Joint Committee on Washington Metropolitan Problems, *Metropolitan Transportation*, by Arthur Lazarus, Joint Committee Print (Washington, D.C.: Government Printing Office, 1958).

9. Ibid., p. 27.

10. Wilbur Smith and Associates, *Mass Transportation Survey, Traffic Engineering Study* (New Haven, Conn.: Wilbur Smith and Associates, 1959).

11. Arthur Lazarus, *Metropolitan Transportation*, p. 16.

12. Ibid.

13. Banks, "Origins of the N.C.T.A.," p. 16.

14. U.S. National Capital Planning Commission and U.S. National Capital Regional Planning Council, *Transportation Plan for the National Capital Region: The Mass Transportation Survey Report—1959* (Washington, D.C.: Government Printing Office, July 1, 1959).

15. Ibid., p. 1.

16. It might be noted that the original auto-dominant plan presented by DeLeuw, Cather & Co. called for 305 miles of freeways and expressways while the "balanced" plan presented to the public called for 329 miles of new roads. U.S. National Capital Planning Commission, Mass Transportation Survey, Joint Steering Committee, *Transcript of Proceedings, July Meeting* (Washington, D.C., July 8, 1958), p. 4.

17. U.S. NCPC and NCRPC, *MTS Report*, pp. 4 and 7.

18. Editorial, *Sunday Star*, July 12, 1959.

19. Editorial, *Washington Post and Times Herald*, July 12, 1959.

20. U.S. NCPC and NCRPC, *MTS Report*, p. 1.

21. Editorial, *Washington Post and Times Herald*, July 12, 1959.

22. Editorial, *Washington Post and Times Herald*, October 12, 1959.

23. Ibid.

24. U.S. Congress, Joint Committee on Washington Metropolitan Problems, *Transportation Plan for the National Capital Region, Hearings*, before the Joint Committee on Washington Metropolitan Problems, Congress of the United States, 86th Cong., 1st Sess., 1959, p. 14.

25. Ibid., pp. 31 and 128.

26. *National Capital Transportation Act of 1960, Statutes at Large*, 74,537 (1960), *U.S. Code*, Vol. 40, sec. 651 (1960).

27. Ibid., sec. 204(a), *Statutes*, 74, 539 (1960), *U.S. Code*, Vol. 40, 664 (1960).

28. Ibid., sec. 204(c), *Statutes*, 74, 540 (1960), *U.S. Code*, Vol. 40, 664 (1960).

29. Ibid., sec. 204(b) (1) & (2), *Statutes*, 74, 539 (1960), *U.S. Code*, Vol. 40, 664 (1960).

30. Ibid., sec. 204 *Statutes*, 74, 537 (1960), *U.S. Code*, Vol. 40, 664 (1960).

31. U.S. Congress, Senate, Committee on the District of Columbia, *Transportation for the National Capital Region*, S. Rept. 1631, To Accompany H.R. 11135, 86th Cong., 2d Sess., 1960, p. 11.

32. Ibid., p. 4.

33. *Transportation Act of 1960, Statutes*, 74, sec. 205(a)(1), 541-542 (1960), *U.S. Code*, Vol. 40, 665, (1960).

34. Senate, *Transportation for National Capital Region*, p. 5.

35. National Capital Transportation Agency, *Transportation in the National Capital Region—Finance and Organization* (Washington, D.C.: Government Printing Office, 1962).

36. Ibid., p. 1.

37. Ibid., p. 31.

38. Ibid., p. 32.

39. See p. 53 above.

40. NCTA, *Transportation in the National Capital*, p. 47.

41. National Capital Transportation Agency, *Appendix to the November, 1962 Report to the President*, Vol. 5 *System Planning* (Washington, D.C.: Government Printing Office, 1963), pp. 97-98.

42. NCTA, *Transportation in the National Capital*, pp. 19-24.

43. Ibid., p. 34.

44. U.S. Congress, House, Committee on the District of Columbia, *Transit Development Program for the National Capital Region*, H. Rept. 1005 To Accompany H.R. 8929, 88th Cong., 1st Sess., 1963, p. 7.

45. Letter from President John F. Kennedy to Vice-President Lyndon B. Johnson (President of the Senate) and Speaker of the House of Representatives John McCormack, May 27, 1963.

46. Quoted from Michael Lash, "Case Study: Conflict in Rapid Transit Planning," in *Urban Mass Transit Planning* ed. Wolfgang S. Homburger (Berkeley, Calif.: University of California, Institute of Transportation and Traffic Engineering, 1967), p. 180.

47. U.S. Congress, House, Committee on the District of Columbia, *Mass Transportation in the District of Columbia*, H. Rept. 2751 To Accompany S. 3073, 84th Cong., 2d Sess., 1956, p. 2. Section 3 of the bill states "no competitive street railway or bus line . . . for the transportation of passengers of the character of which runs over a fixed route on a fixed schedule, shall be established to operate in the District of Columbia. . . ."

48. House, *Transit Development Program*, H. Rept. 1005.

49. Ibid., p. 7.

50. Ibid., p. 9. What the committee apparently chose to ignore in rejecting the regional system proposed by the NCTA was that such a transit system could heavily influence the direction and quality of regional growth.

51. U.S. Congress, House, 88th Cong., 1st Sess., December 9, 1963, *Congressional Record*, 109, 23872.

52. Ibid., p. 23860.

53. Ibid., pp. 23862-23863.

54. Editorial, *Washington Post and Times Herald*, December 11, 1963.

55. The interpretation of congressional intention was made by Michael Lash, "Conflict in Rapid Transit Planning," p. 182, but is also clearly evident in the debate on the measure.

56. Committee on Washington Metropolitan Problems, *Transportation Plan*, hearings, pp. 236-237.

57. U.S. Congress, House, Committee for the District of Columbia, *Transit Program for the National Capital Region, Hearings*, before subcommittee No. 6 of the Committee on the District of Columbia, House of Representatives, on H.R. 6633 and H.R. 7240, 88th Cong., 1st Sess., 1963, pp. 263-264.

Notes to Chapter 4

1. *The National Capital Transportation Act of 1965, Statutes at Large*, 79, 664 (1965), *U.S. Code*, Vol. 40, sec. 682 (1965).

2. National Capital Transportation Agency, *Rail Rapid Transit for the Nation's Capital–Transit Development Program, 1965* (Washington, D.C.: Government Printing Office, 1965).

3. Ibid., p. 25.

4. *Transportation Act of 1965*, *Statutes*, 79, sec. 3(b)(3), 664 (1965), *U.S. Code*, Vol. 40, 682 (1965).

5. This section is based on Lash, "Conflict in Rapid Transit Planning," p. 183.

6. Editorial, *Washington Post and Times Herald*, September 10, 1966.

7. U.S. Congress, Senate, *Washington Metropolitan Area Transit Authority Compact*, 89th Cong., 2d Sess., 1966, S. 3488.

8. Ibid., article 2, sec. 2.

9. Ibid., article 15, sec. 51.

10. Ibid., article 16, sec. 86(3)(c).

11. U.S. Congress, House, Committee on the District of Columbia, *Amend the National Capital Transportation Act of 1965, Hearings*, before subcommittee No. 4 of the Committee on the District of Columbia, House of Representatives, on H.R. 11,395, 90th Cong., 1st Sess., 1967, p. 2.

12. Ibid., p. 2.

13. Ibid., p. 4.

14. NCTA, *Transportation in the National Capital*, p. 58.

15. U.S. Congress, Senate, Committee on the District of Columbia, *Amend the National Capital Transportation Act of 1965, Hearings*, before the Committee on the District of Columbia, Senate, on S. 2094 and H.R. 11395, 90th Cong., 1st Sess., 1967, p. 54.

16. House, *Amend the National Capital Transportation Act of 1965*, p. 66.

17. Ibid.

18. NCTA, *Transportation in the National Capital*, p. 56.

19. Senate, *Amend the National Capital Transportation Act of 1965*, p. 73.

20. Ibid., p. 56.

21. Richard Severo, "Potomac Watch," *Washington Post and Times Herald*, March 15, 1967.

22. Ibid.

23. House, *Amend the National Capital Transportation Act of 1965*, p. 61.

24. U.S. Congress, House, Rep. Bingham speaking against amending the National Capital Transportation Act of 1965, H.R. 11395, 90th Cong., 1st Sess., October 9, 1967, *Congressional Record*, 113, 28156.

25. James E. Clayton, "Lessons for METRO in San Francisco," *Washington Post and Times Herald*, January 11, 1970.

26. Robert L. Morris, *Preliminary Regional System Planning Report*, presented to the WMATA Board of Directors (Washington, D.C.: Office of Planning and Finance, WMATA, 1967), p. 2.

27. Richard H. Pratt, *Considerations in Rail Rapid Transit Route Planning*, presented to the WMATA Board of Directors (Washington, D.C.: Office of Planning and Finance, WMATA, 1967), p. 2.

28. Ibid., p. 5.

29. Richard H. Pratt, private interview held in Bethesda, Maryland, January 2, 1970.

30. Senate, *Transit Authority Compact*, article 16, sec. 86(3)(c).

31. U.S. Congress, Senate, Committee on the District of Columbia, *General Information Relating to the Committee on the District of Columbia Together with the Origin and Form of the Government of the District of Columbia*, Committee Print, 91st Cong., 1st Sess., 1969, pp. 4-5.

32. *Highway Act of 1968, Statutes at Large*, 82 sec. 23, 847 (1968).

33. *Washington Post and Times Herald*, August 12, 1969, p. A-1.

34. Ibid.

35. Ibid.

36. Ibid., September 25, 1969, p. A-13.

37. Ibid.

38. Joint Committee on Washington Metropolitan Problems, *MTS Survey Plan*, p. 586.

39. Ibid., p. 587.

40. Ibid.

41. U.S. Congress, House and Senate, *Financing Subway System for National Capital Region, Hearings*, before the Committee on the District of Columbia and Subcommittee No. 4 of the Committees on the District of Columbia, Senate and House of Representatives, on S. 2185 and H.R. 11,193, 91st Cong., 1st Sess., 1969, p. 88.

Notes to Chapter 5

1. Charles E. Lindblom, *The Policy-Making Process* (Englewood Cliffs, N.J.: Prentice Hall, 1968), p. 13.

2. Edward C. Banfield, *Political Influence* (Glencoe, Ill.: The Free Press, 1961), p. 329.

3. Ibid.

4. Lindblom, *The Policy-Making Process*, pp. 24-25.

5. Ibid.

6. Eugene Eidenberg, "The Presidency: Americanizing the War in Vietnam," in *American Political Institutions and Public Policy*, ed. Allan P. Sindler (Boston: Little, Brown and Company, 1969), pp. 69, 91-95, and 116-123.

7. Banfield, *Political Influence*, p. 330.

8. Ibid.

9. U.S. Congress, House, Committee on the District of Columbia, *Transit Program for the National Capital Region, Hearings*, before a subcommittee of the Committee on the District of Columbia, House of Representatives, on H.R. 6633 and H.R. 7240, 88th Cong., 1st Sess., 1963, p. 58.

10. Richard H. Pratt, *Considerations in Rail Rapid Transit Route Planning*, presented to the WMATA Board of Directors (Washington, D.C.: Office of Planning and Finance, WMATA, 1967), p. 8.

11. Larry Smith & Company, *Use of Excess Land and Air Rights*, prepared for the National Capital Transportation Agency (Washington, D.C., August, 1962). Anthony Downs has noted of the impact of new transportation arteries on land values that a ". . . transit artery extending outward from the center of a metropolitan area through outlying areas where rapid growth is occurring . . . will normally have the greatest potential impact on land values." "The Land-Value Impacts of Transportation Arteries and How They Affect New City Development," in *Urban Problems and Prospects*, ed. Anthony Downs (Chicago: Markham Publishing Company, 1970), p. 234.

12. Walter W. Washington, Mayor of Washington, D.C., Remarks at the Groundbreaking Ceremonies of METRO, December 9, 1969, p. 2.

13. National Capital Transportation Agency, *Transportation in the National Capital Region—Finance and Organization* (Washington, D.C.: U.S. Government Printing Office, 1962), p. 58.